James Shirrefs

An inquiry into the life, writings and character of the Reverend

Doctor William Guild

James Shirrefs

An inquiry into the life, writings and character of the Reverend Doctor William Guild

ISBN/EAN: 9783743355224

Manufactured in Europe, USA, Canada, Australia, Japa

Cover: Foto ©ninafisch / pixelio.de

Manufactured and distributed by brebook publishing software (www.brebook.com)

James Shirrefs

An inquiry into the life, writings and character of the Reverend

Doctor William Guild

AN INQUIRY

INTO THE

LIFE OF DR. GUILD.

AN
INQUIRY

INTO THE

LIFE, WRITINGS, AND CHARACTER,

OF THE REVEREND

DOCTOR *WILLIAM GUILD,*

ONE OF THE CHAPLAINS IN ORDINARY TO HIS MAJESTY
KING CHARLES I,
AND
FOUNDER OF THE TRINITY HOSPITAL, ABERDEEN.

WITH SOME STRICTURES UPON

SPALDING'S ACCOUNT OF HIM,

AND OF THE TIMES IN WHICH HE LIVED.

BY
JAMES SHIRREFS, D. D.

SENIOR MINISTER OF ABERDEEN,
AND PATRON OF THE INCORPORATED TRADES.

Still in thy right Hand carry gentle Peace,
To silence envious Tongues.   Be just, and fear not:
Let all the Ends thou aim'st at, be thy Country's,
Thy God's, and Truth's; then, if thou fall'st—
Thou fall'st a blessed Martyr.

THE SECOND EDITION, ENLARGED.

ABERDEEN:

PRINTED FOR AND SOLD BY A. ANGUS AND SON; A. BROWN; AND
J. BURNETT; F. AND C. RIVINGTON, LONDON; P. HILL;
AND A. CONSTABLE, EDINBURGH.

MDCCXCIX.

INCORPORATED TRADES

OF

ABERDEEN.

———

WHEN I entered on the Inquiry, the result of which I now prefent to you, I forefaw fome difficulties in the way, which were not to be eafily furmounted.

To form an impartial fketch of the life and character of Dr. Guild was impoffible, from any thing tranfmitted to us concern-

ing

ing him, by the Public Hiſtorians of the eventful period, in which he lived. A teſtimony, apparently given under the influence of ſtubborn prejudice, like that of Spalding, who has endeavoured to blaſt the reputation of this eminent man, was not much to be truſted. It was not, however, to be peremptorily rejected, without ſufficient evidence of its being falſe. The grounds of bold aſſertions were to be examined, and facts aſcertained beyond a doubt, by recourſe to Authentic Records, and to every other ſource of faithful information.

The object I had in view was important, and worth much trouble. It was not merely to gratify curioſity, but to do juſtice to a character, of ſome undeniable excellence; and to clear it, from the aſperſions of petulant obloquy. How far my en-

endeavours have been fuccefsful, I leave to the judgment of others.

Of the fketch here given, I fhall only fay, that if it be erroneous, in any refpect, it is not wilfully fo. It has been drawn from authorities generally accounted credible; and it refts on proofs, which are feldom fuppofed to be fallacious.

To You, the Incorporated Trades of Aberdeen, for whofe perufal it was chiefly intended, I know, it will be acceptable, as a tribute of refpect to the memory of one, whom you have juft caufe to honour; and as a mark of attention to your wifhes, from

Your affectionate Friend,

And Patron,

JAMES SHIRREFS.

ADVER-

ADVERTISEMENT to the SECOND EDITION.

THE subject of detail in the following sheets is, in a certain degree, limited and local.—Some persons, however, who have perused them, and on whose judgment the Author would, in most cases, rely more than on his own, have suggested that the memoirs they contain may be acceptable to many readers, who have no particular connexion with the place, where the scene of Dr. Guild's beneficence lay.

In deference to this opinion, and that those who applied for copies, after the former edition was sold off, might not be disappointed, a new edition of the Inquiry into the Life of Dr. GUILD, is presented to the public.

AN

AN INQUIRY, &c.

"I HAVE often thought," fays a celebrated writer, " that there has rarely paf-
" fed a life, of which a judicious and
" faithful narrative would not be ufeful."
In this fentiment, many will entirely agree;
and, of thofe who have formed an opinion fomewhat different, few will refufe
to acknowledge, that the page of Biogra-

phy,

phy, as a record of thofe who have me-
rited the honours of a lafting name, is too
feldom devoted to the lives of Literary
Men.

It is full of the intrigues of Courtiers,
the fchemes of Statefmen, and the exploits
of Warriours; while it rarely celebrates
the refearches of the Philofopher, or the
humble labours of the Divine.

Yet he, whofe life, however devoid of
varied incident, has been fpent in extend-
ing the boundaries of Science, or the empire of Truth, is furely more worthy to
be had in remembrance, than the mini-
ons of Princes, or the cruel ravagers of
countries.

Whatever has any reference to the life
and character of fuch a man, will be acceptable and interefting to thofe, who ad-
mire genius, or who love virtue. Even
the

the fimple record of his name and parentage; the education he received; the ftation he occupied; and the benevolence he difplayed; will be gratifying to pofterity, while there remains, in human fociety, any reverence for the memory of its brighteft ornaments, and moft eftimable friends.

The reverend Divine, of whom my inquiry has traced the following Memoirs, was the fon, and, it feems probable, the only fon, of an eminent artificer in Aberdeen. He had three fifters, (Jean, Chriftian, and Margaret) two of whom furvived him, and fucceeded to a part of his eftate. *Jean* was married to David Anderfon of Finzeauch, celebrated in the Statiftical Account of Aberdeen, as fo eminent for his Philofophical knowledge and abilities, that he was commonly called *Davie do a'thing.* She died before her bro-

B 2

ther,

ther, and bequeathed a very confiderable fum, " for the maintenance and education " of poor orphans." *Chriftian* was unmarried, at the time of her brother's death. *Margaret*, the other furviving fifter, was married to Thomas Cufhnie, Glazier.

The names of fome of Mr. Guild's other relations and kinfmen are alfo tranfmitted to us; but if he ever had a brother, there is no mention of him, in any record or paper from which information concerning his family could be expected.

In Aberdeen, the place of his nativity, there is not a public regifter of births or baptifms, of fo ancient a date as the year *one thoufand five hundred and eighty fix.* It is, however, fufficiently afcertained, by other authentic evidence, that he was born in *that year*, though the particular day of his birth cannot now be known.

His

His father, *Matthew Guild*, was a member of the Corporation of Hammermen. Being one of thofe who were called *Armourers*, and induſtrious in his profeſſion, it was not extraordinary if he attained opulence, at a time when there were few articles fo much in demand as arms. He was able, it is certain, to fupport his family decently, and to afford his fon the advantage of a liberal education.

The young man was accordingly placed under the care of proper teachers, as foon as he could profit by inſtruction; and his progreſs, in the common rudiments of learning, was fuch as to qualify him early for fomething higher. Fortunately he had not far to go, for the neceſſary means of further improvement. The *New College* of Aberdeen, as it was then called, founded by George Earl *Marifchal*, had been

B 3   lately

lately opened for the reception of ſtudents. A conſiderable number had been admitted, and ſeveral claſſes regularly formed, when *William Guild* was entered to this ſeminary.

He had here an opportunity of ſtudying under a few learned men, all the uſual branches of academical ſcience. It is highly probable, that he applied with much diligence and ſucceſs, to his ſtudies in general; but that which he ſeems to have reliſhed moſt, and to which he peculiarly devoted himſelf, was Theology.

The want of a Profeſſor of Divinity, in the New College, appears, at this time, to have been ſupplied, by ſome one of the Profeſſors already eſtabliſhed. Perhaps the ſtudents had alſo, as they now have, the privilege of attending the theological lectures, given in like manner, in the neighbouring

bouring Univerſity; for even in King's College, a particular endowment for ſuch lectures had not yet been made.

The proficiency of Mr. Guild, by whomſoever his ſtudies in theology were conducted, did great honour to his maſters. Scarcely had the time elapſed, which ordinarily paſſes in the obſcurity of juvenile years, when he became known to the public, as an author. At the age of twenty two, he publiſhed a treatiſe, entitled, *The new Sacrifice of Chriſtian Incenſe; or, the true Entry to the Tree of Life, and Gracious Gate of glorious Paradiſe.*

This book, printed at London in the year 1608, was dedicated " to the amiable " Prince *Henry*, to *Charles* Duke of York, " and to the Princeſs *Elizabeth*;" the unfortunate family of King *James I.* whoſe future days were far from being ſo proſ-

perous

perous, as thofe of their youth had feemed to forebode.

It is impoffible now, to trace the feries **of Mr.** Guild's works. There are, however, obvious reafons for thinking, that this was his firft production. His next, was a little work, which he publifhed the fame year, under the title of *The only Way to Salvation ; or, the Life and Soul of true Religion.* This book alfo was printed at London.

The national prejudice of the *Englifh* againft the *Scots,* which, about this time, many things had concurred to inflame, might have tempted a writer, lefs attached to his country **than Mr** Guild, to **conceal** the circumftance of his having been born on the *north fide* of the *Tweed.*

But our author had no defire to pafs for what he was not ; and announced without

re-

referve, on his firft performance, that it came from the pen of a *Scotchman*.

How different was the conduct of *Mallet* the poet! Of him it is faid, that, having cleared his tongue from his native pronunciation, fo as to be no longer diftinguifhed as a Scot, he feemed inclined to difencumber himfelf from all adherences of his original, and took upon him to change his name, from Scotch *Malloch* to Englifh *Mallet*, without any imaginable reafon of preference, which the eye or ear can difcover. This is remarked by Dr. *Samuel Johnfon*, a writer nowife partial towards *Scotland*, as an inftance of Mallet's difrefpect to his native country, of which the Doctor could not approve. It was certainly a puerile affectation, unworthy of an ingenuous mind, and exhibits a ftriking contraft to the manly franknefs of Mr. Guild.

Both

Both the treatifes I have mentioned appear to have been written, before he had
entered into holy orders. No mark, deno-
ting the clerical **character**, is annexed to
his name, on either of them; while, in his
fubfequent publications, it is commonly
accompanied, among other marks of diftinction, with the venerable addition of
Minifter of God's Word.

It is not always fortunate for an author
to meet with high approbation, on his firft
effay. Nothing has a more pernicious influence on rifing genius, than extravagant
and univerfal praife. Elated by unexpec-
ted and unufual fuccefs, the young adven-
turer for literary **fame** is apt to over-rate
his abilities; to write too much, and to
publifh too haftily.

Mr. Guild, though abundantly fuccefsful, had ftill the good fenfe to avoid thefe

errors

errors. His writings were neither volu-
minous, nor fuperficial; but judicioufly
concife; and confined to fubjects which
he was well qualified to difcufs. Of this
character, at leaft, are all his performances,
which the writer of thefe memoirs has had
accefs to fee. It may be added, that however favourably his tracts, in 1608, were received, he did not, for more than ten years
after, offer any other effay to the public.

The commencement of his miniftry was
of the fame date, with that of his reputation as an author.

It was in the year one thoufand fix hundred and eight, that he was called to the
paftoral charge of the parifh of King-Edward, in the prefbytery of Turriff, and
fynod of Aberdeen. Here, in rural quiet,
little apprehenfive of the ftorms he had afterwards to encounter, he paffed fome of

his

his happieſt years. Amidſt the laborious duties of his office, in a pariſh of confiderable extent, he had the ſupport of a mind confcious of doing good, and the ſtrong encouragement of a grateful people.

The tender endearments of conjugal affection were added to his other comforts, by his marriage to Mrs. *Katharine Rowen*, daughter of — Rowen, or Rolland, of Diſblair, which took place in the year 1610. As they had no children, he knew not the cares, nor the pleaſures of a father; but, he had cares of another kind, in which this amiable woman was deſtined to ſhare, and which her ſweet ſociety helped him to ſuſtain.

The particulars of the life of a man of any eminence, cannot poſſibly be ſtated, without incidental mention of the conduct of other perſons, with whom he was connected;

nected; and of the public tranfactions of the age, in which he lived. Mr. Guild had not been long Minifter at King-Edward, when his prudence and abilities became neceffary in affairs of much greater magnitude than thofe of his parochial charge.

King *James*, from his acceffion to the throne of England, had formed a defign of bringing the Scottifh clergy to an entire conformity to the Englifh church. Proceeding, at firft, with the moft wary circumfpection, and nice difcernment; obferving the proper time; foothing, and giving way, when he perceived it to be neceffary; he had procured, in the year 1610, the introduction of a kind of epifcopacy into Scotland. But as there was no liturgy, and as the Bifhops had little more of power, or of revenue, than the inferior clergy;

clergy; the King was very defirous of having this defect fupplied, and of eftablifhing Epifcopacy, in its full authority and luftre. [A]

Accordingly, in the year 1617, after fourteen years abfence from Scotland, he refolved to vifit that kingdom; that he might try, in perfon, what could be done, for the advancement of his favourite fcheme. He was attended, on this vifit, by a fuitable retinue; but by no perfon, more juftly deferving of refpect, than Dr. *Lancelot Andrews*, Bifhop of Ely; who was one of the Privy Council of England, and was alfo, on this occafion, named a Privy Counfellor for Scotland. To this worthy Prelate, for whom he had the higheft efteem, K. *James* committed the management of the delicate and important bufinefs, which his Majefty had fo much at heart;

heart; and, **in** which if any one could have been fuccefsful, it would have been the learned, the pious, and the meek *Bifhop Andrews.*

The firft ftep, which **his** prudence fuggefted, was to confult the moft eminent of the clergy of Scotland. Among **thefe, he** particularly diftinguifhed **Mr. Guild**, by marks of uncommon attention and regard. Though the King had been obliged to **defift** from an attempt, to reftore the Bifhops and Chapters to their temporalities, a National Synod had, under **the royal autho**rity, lately been held at Aberdeen, with a view to the eftablifhment of a public liturgy. Of this Affembly **the Archbifhop** of St. Andrews fat as Moderator, and his Majefty's Commiffioner was the Earl of Montrofe. What concern Mr. Guild took, on the occafion, does not clearly appear.

pear. It is not improbable, that the meafure propofed had his approbation ; and
the decifion of the Synod was favourable.
A liturgy was deemed **ex**pedient, and appointed to be prepared, as foon **as** poffible,
for the ufe of all the kingdom.

In this ftate of things, the conciliatory
manner and moderation of Dr. *Andrews*
had furmounted many obftacles, when the
zeal and impatience of the King aroufed,
by fome ungracious acts, a latent fpirit of
difcontent and oppofition, which made it
abfolutely neceffary to abandon the project.
Nor was there any thing of the kind again
attempted, during the reign of *James*.

In the year 1618, Bifhop *Andrews* was
promoted to the See of Winchefter, and
Mr. Guild foon after dedicated to him, a
treatife which he publifhed, under the title
of *Mofes Unveiled*.

The

The defign of this work, as the author himfelf informs us, is to " explain thofe " figures which ferved unto the pattern " and fhadow of heavenly things, pointing " out the Meffiah *Chrift Jefus*."

Of the character and merits of the good Bifhop, to whom it is infcribed, Mr. **Guild** fpeaks with much affection and refpect.

Seldom, indeed, is the tribute of dedicatory praife fo properly beftowed, as it was here. Few have been thought to deferve, and not many have obtained, a more liberal portion of panegyric than Dr. Andrews.

But as a clearer infight into the character of a great man is often procured, by little incidents, or cafual and unpremeditated remarks, than in any other way, judicious and penetrating writers are found to record fome things very carefully, which to men of lefs difcernment may appear unimpor-

tant

tant and trivial. A circumftance of this
nature is left on record, concerning **Andrews**, which gives a ftrong impreffion of
his character. On the day, when K. *James*
had fuddenly diffolved the Parliament, becaufe not fo obfequious as he wifhed, his
Majefty, while dining in ftate, faid to the
Bifhops of *Durham* and *Winchefter*, who
were ftanding by his chair, " My Lords,
" cannot I take my fubjects' money, when
" I want it, without all this formality in
" Parliament ?" *Neale*, Bifhop of Durham, a
fawning courtier, readily anfwered, " God
" **forbid**, Sir, but you fhould; you are
" the breath of our noftrils. " Whereupon
the King turned, and faid to the Bifhop of
Winchefter, " Well, my Lord, what fay
" you ?" " Sir," replied *Andrews*, modeftly,
" I have no fkill to judge of Parliamentary
" cafes." The King anfwered, " No put-
" offs,

" offs, my Lord, anſwer me preſently."
" Then, Sir," ſaid he, " I think it lawful
" for you to take my brother Neale's mo-
" ney, for he offers it." It is not very dif-
ficult to conjecture, how the King would
reliſh this anſwer. We are told, that he
ſeemed to be diſpleaſed ; but he made no
reply. Which of the two Biſhops was moſt
deſerving of the favour and confidence of
his Sovereign, the reader is left to judge.

The friendſhip of a man of ſuch inflexi-
ble integrity, and independence of ſpirit,
as Biſhop *Andrews,* was an acquiſition of
great value ; and Mr. Guild had the happineſs to enjoy it, from the commencement of their acquaintance to the end of
the Biſhop's life. His death, which happened in the year 1626, was lamented, in
an elegant Latin Elegy written by *Milton,*

and

and preferved among the works of that ad-
mirable poet.

The fame circumftances, which gave rife
to Mr. Guild's intimacy with Bifhop Andrews, brought him alfo another very refpectable and learned friend, in Dr. *Young*,
a countryman of his own, who was Dean
of Winchefter.   By means of this gentleman, who was in high favour at court, he
had the honour of being introduced to the
King, and was afterwards appointed to be
one of his Majefty's Chaplains.   His obligations to Dr. Young he acknowledges,
in a dedication to him, prefixed to a fcrip-
tural piece, called, *The Harmony of all the
Prophets* ; which appears to have been
publifhed in the beginning of the reign of
his royal Patron, King *Charles* the firft.

His object, in this performance, was, by
a view

a view of the prophecies concerning the Mefliah, " to confirm the Chriftian, and " convince the Jew."

His *Mofes Unveiled*, and his *Harmony of the Prophets*, were neither the largeft, nor the moft elaborate, of Mr. Guild's works; but they were certainly the moft popular of all his performances. Like his other treatifes, they are now become fcarce, though feveral editions of them were publifhed, at different times, both in Scotland and England.

As his attention to public matters did not prevent him from applying diligently to his private ftudies, he continued, during his refidence at King-Edward, to exercife his talent for compofition, and occafionally fent to the prefs fome ufeful tracts. Moft of his performances were of the popular kind, and all of them appear to have

C 3

been

been adapted, as much as poffible, to common ufe; but his literary merit was acknowledged by thofe, who were more
competent judges than the multitude.
Men of learning knew him to be learned;
the academical honour of Doctor in Divinity was conferred upon him; and he was
ranked, while yet a young man, among the
ableft divines in the Church of Scotland.

The Reformation from *Popery*, had occafioned a variety of theological controverfies, in which the *Proteftant* clergy exerted themfelves, with great vigour and
fuccefs; and, to their immortal honour,
brought together an invincible collection
of arguments, againft the corruptions and
errors of the *Romifh Church*. Dr. Guild
ftood forth, with his brethren of the reformed churches, in fupport of the common
caufe.

On

On the fide of Popery, one of the acuteft writers was, the celebrated Cardinal *Bellarmin*, an Italian Jefuit, who did great honour to his order. He, though a ftrenuous advocate for the Romifh religion, did by no means agree with the doctrine of the Jefuits, in every point; nor approve of feveral expreffions in their Litanies: and was, upon the whole, more candid and liberal than any other of the Romifh writers.

Among the Romanifts there were fome, who accufed him of undermining the fabric, which he was very fkilfully endeavouring to prop.

But the Proteftants had fo much refpect for his learning and abilities, and accounted his publications fo deferving of the fulleft reply, that, for a period of near fifty years, there was fcarcely any eminent di-

vine,

vine amongſt them, who did not write againſt Bellarmin.

We cannot, therefore, be ſurpriſed to find Dr. Guild among the number of his antagoniſts. In the year 1625, he publiſhed a polemical work, entitled, *Ignis Fatuus; or, the Elf-fire of Purgatory:* wherein Bellarmin is confuted, by arguments both out of the Old and New Teſtament, and by his own proofs out of the ſcriptures and fathers.

The title of this book may be thought ſomewhat fantaſtical, but it was ſuited to the taſte and genius of the age. They, who are, in any meaſure, acquainted with the writings of that period, know that ſimilar titles were then very common, and given to the performances of many of the moſt judicious and learned writers.

An

An *Annex to this Treatife of Purgatory*, concerning the diftinction of fin into *Mortal* and *Venial*, was afterwards publifhed by Dr. Guild; and dedicated to the *Earl* and *Countefs* of *Lauderdale*, who had a better claim to fuch a compliment than high rank or opulence could give.

The fuccefs of this fpecimen of his abilities, in the field of controverfy, appears to have encouraged him to further exertions. For, his treatife on the *Purgatory* of the Romifh Church, was foon followed by another, which he publifhed in the year 1626, on her pretenfions to *Antiquity*.

This work, which he entitled *Popifh glorying in Antiquity turned to their Shame,* was dedicated to *Sir Alexander Gordon* of Cluny, Baronet; and was defigned, the Doctor tells us, to fhow " how that where-" unto they pretend to carry greateft re-
" verence,

" verence, they wrong, vilify, and dif-
" grace; and are moft guilty of that which
" they upbraid to others."

Whatever he had hitherto publifhed,
had been printed at London. His next
publication came from the prefs of *Ed-
ward Raban* at Aberdeen. It was called
A Compend of the Controverfies of Religion,
and dedicated to the *Countefs of Einzie*.

But the peaceful retirement of the country, fo favourable to his ftudies, was now
foon to be exchanged for a fituation, in
which they were to fuffer a long and fad
interruption. His virtues, and his talents,
were to have other trials; and he appears
little more as a writer, for near twenty
years.

On the ninth of December 1629, one
of the paftoral charges in Aberdeen became vacant, by the voluntary refignation

of

of Mr James Rofs, on account of his age and infirmities. The Magiftrates and Council, defirous to fhow every mark of refpect and gratitude to their retiring paftor, who had been thirty years in that important office, were in no hafte to fill up the vacancy; and beftowed on Mr. Rofs a very liberal pecuniary prefent, that nothing, on their part, might be wanting to his fupport and comfort, in the decline of life.

At laft, when they found it neceffary to elect another paftor, their choice was naturally fixed, on their townfman Doctor Guild; who was appointed fucceffor to Mr. Rofs, on the twelfth of January 1631. The record of his election bears honourable teftimony to his character and abilities; and ftates, as the reafons for his being chofen, his " having preached in
" the

" the pulpits of the town, feveral times,
" to the contentment and general applaufe
" of the whole congregation, and withal
" knowing him to be a man of learning,
" good life and converfation*."

The diocefs of Aberdeen was, at that
time, under the infpection of *Bifhop Forbes*
of Corfe, a man of great fanctity, and of
apoftolic vigilance and concern for thofe
committed to his care. He is faid to have
been peculiarly attentive, to the parochial
vacancies in New and Old Aberdeen, the
metropolis of the county, and the feat of
the univerfity; and to have employed his
influence, in fupplying them with Minifters, who were eminently qualified to be
ufeful, in fuch a fituation. How far the
election of Dr. Guild was forwarded, by
his recommendation or advice, cannot now

* Council Regifter, Aberdeen, 1631.

be

be known. That it had his concurrence and approbation, there is good reafon to believe. It called to one of thofe ftations in his diocefs, in which he was folicitous to place men of diftinguifhed merit, a perfon, in every refpect, fuch as the worthy dio- cefan could have wifhed.

Doctor Guild, having confented to this election, was removed from King-Edward to Aberdeen, by the ufual procedure of his ecclefiaftical fuperiours. In his new fituation, he was not likely to have much leifure, but he had a reafonable profpect of being ufeful and happy. He was very acceptable to the people committed to his care; and he was joined to colleagues who were, like himfelf, pious, moderate, and learned men. His colleagues were Doctor William Forbes, Doctor James Sibbald, and Doctor Alexander Rofs; of whom Dr.
Sib-

Sibbald, though a man of some eminence, was perhaps the least remarkable. The other two were men, not indubitably of greater abilities than Dr. Sibbald, but of greater fame.

Dr. Forbes was the preacher, whom King *Charles*, when he had heard him, complimented so highly as to say, that he " was worthy of having a Bishopric erected " for him;" a compliment, the more deserving of notice, as his Majesty followed it, with the erection of the diocese of Edinburgh (on the twenty ninth of September 1633) and appointed Dr. Forbes to be its Bishop. The text of this so much admired discourse, we are told, was the twenty seventh verse of the fourteenth chapter of the gospel according to St. John, *Peace I leave with you, my peace I give unto you; not as the world giveth, give I unto you. Let*

not

not your heart be troubled, neither let it be afraid.

Dr. Rofs was the well-known author of a work, entitled *Panfebeia, or a View of all Religions*, and the perfon to whom the facetious poet, who gave us *Hudibras*, has been faid to allude, in the following lines.

There was an ancient fage Philofopher,
That had read *Alexander Rofs* over;
And fwore the world, as he could prove,
Was made of fighting, and of love.

But, however defervedly Hudibras has been applauded, as a compofition of wit and humour, one cannot always approve the tendency of what that poem contains, nor admit the juftnefs of the fatire. " Pro-" per *fatire*," fays a very able critic, " is " diftinguifhed, by the generality of the " reflections, from a *lampoon*, which is aim-" ed againft a particular perfon." In the inftance

inftance before us, the attack could not poffibly be more indelicate, or more perfonal, I had almoft faid, more malicious. Whatever were the defects of Dr. Rofs as a writer, he was refpectable as a man; and, a man of fenfe and learning, notwithftanding the ludicrous allufion, by which *Butler* hath difhonoured him.

Such were the colleagues, with whom Dr. Guild was affociated, in the work of the Miniftry at Aberdeen. He was foon deprived of Dr. Forbes, as a colleague, by his promotion to the See of Edinburgh. But he continued to enjoy the affiftance of Dr. Sibbald and Dr. Rofs, until the troubles which afterwards arofe forced all the three to withdraw from their charge, to which Dr. Rofs never returned.

His willing acceptance of an invitation to be one of their paftors, was not the

only

only proof, which Dr. Guild gave to the citizens of Aberdeen, of his difinterefted attachment to them, and his anxious defire to promote their happinefs. Their public feminaries of learning, and their focieties for the encouragement of honeft induftry, found in him an early, generous, and fteady friend. Many years before he had any profpect of leaving the parifh of King-Edward, he became a benefactor to Aberdeen.

In the year 1623, he had given to the Town Council, a donation of a Houfe, which he had purchafed, for the laudable purpofe of enabling them to enlarge and improve the gateway of Marifchal college. This was probably the firft public act of his munificence. To the community, that houfe was, from its fituation, of more than ordinary value. It was in the vici-

D   nity

nity of the Gray Friars Church, as well as
of the college; and the ground on which
it ftood was capable of being employed,
much to the advantage of both thefe venerable buildings. That it fhould be fo employed, was what the worthy Donor had in
view, and what the Council exprefsly un-
dertook. But however faithfully they ful-
filled their engagement, unfortunately the
Gray Friars Church was found to be in
need of more improvement, than its fhare
of this little fund could afford.

The Gray Friars Church had been built
by Bifhop Gavin Dunbar, and occafionally
repaired by others, without any expence
to the public. But, the contributions from
private perfons having failed, and the public funds being, it would feem, unable to
fupply the want, this church, when it became next an object of Dr. Guild's attention,

tion, about ten years after his former donation, was in such a ſtate as to be unfit
for the purpoſe of divine ſervice. Being
grieved to ſee it ſo much neglected, he
contributed liberally towards its reparation.
By his bounty, with a ſmall aid from another benevolent citizen (Mr. Alexander
Stewart, Merchant) all its windows were
glazed, in 1633; and it was again opened
for public worſhip, after it had lain waſte
ſeveral years.

In the year 1640, when the General
Aſſembly convened at Aberdeen, the Gray
Friars Church was commodious enough
to be fixed upon as the place, where they
held all their meetings. And, from the
time of its being repaired by Dr. Guild to
the preſent day, the managers of the public funds have, much to their honour, found
means to ſupport ſufficiently this ancient

fabric.

fabric, without any such encroachments upon private charity.

The next, and the greateft, of Dr. **Guild's** public donations, was given to the Incorporated Trades of Aberdeen.

As there are many advantages refulting from the focial union of men engaged in the fame ufeful profeffion, corporations of fuch perfons have been formed and encouraged, in all civilized countries. A confiderable number of artificers and others have been fo united in Aberdeen, under royal charters of different, and fome of them of very ancient dates. It was long, however, **before** they had, as a **fociety,** any competent provifion for the relief **of thofe** among them, who might be reduced to a ftate of indigence. The chief honour of fupplying this want, was referved for Dr. Guild ; **to** whom the incorporations of

Aber-

Aberdeen are, on many accounts, under very great obligations.

Of this fociety, in which there are feven United Corporations, one of the eftablifhed Minifters of Aberdeen, is elected *Patron*, and invefted with certain powers of Superintendence and Guardianfhip, in the management of their affairs. Doctor Guild perhaps was not the firft, to whom fuch powers had been committed; but, when he became Patron, the Corporations received from him, fo liberal an addition to their common funds, that he has juftly been confidered as the perfon, who laid the foundation of their refpectability and opulence.

Over the gateway of an ancient building, which he appropriated for an hofpital to Indigent Artificers, are three ornamented pannels; placed there by the

Corporations, in public acknowledgment of his munificence. [B]

In the higheſt part of the ornamental work, are the words *Soli Deo Gloria*, encircling the date 1632.

On the pannels, are the following inſcriptions,

I.

Fundavit Gulielm' R. Scot. 1181.

Under the Imperial Crown and enſigns armorial of the kingdom, appear the words,

> *To yᵉ. glorie of God*
> *And comfort of the Poore*
> *This Hows was given*
> *To the Crafts by Mr. Wiliam*
> *Guild Doctour of Divinitie*
> *miniſter of Abd:* 1633.

II.

II.

Around the Family Arms of Doctor Guild, the letters

D.

W.   *G.*

Fundator.

III.

He . That . Pitieth . The . Poore . Lendeth .
To . The . Lord . And . That . Which . He .
Hath . Given . Will . He . Repay . Prov.
19. 17.

In the records of the Convener-Court, for the year 1632, it is mentioned, that "Doctor William Guild, Pastor of Aber- "deen, and Patron of the Traids of the "said burgh, did mortify and bestow se- "veral annuities and casualities; and in "particular did bestow somewhat freely, "in assisting the foresaid Traids, to build "and repair their Meeting-house [Hall]

D 4   "and

" and Chapel, and for that effect did ap-
" poynt, that a faithful, chriftian, honeft
" man (one of the faid traids) fhall be
" chofen yearlie, by advice of the patron,
" and his fucceffors, as patrons, with con-
" fent of the members of the Deacon Con-
" veiner Court, to collect the whole rents
" and cafualities belonging thereto, as he
" fhall be appoynted, by the acts made or
" to be made thereanent." But the deed
of foundation, refpecting the Trades Hofpital, was not completely formed, nor ratified by royal charter, until the month of
June 1633.

The preamble of that deed is expreffive
enough, of the motives and defign of the
pious founder. " *Wit ye me*, to the glory
" of God, comfort of the needy, and good
" example of others, charity towards the
" poor, whom our Lord Jefus Chrift to
                   " the

" the end of the world left amongſt us, to
" be nouriſhed, clothed, and fed, to have
" founded, gifted, and perpetually morti-
" fied to the poor tradeſmen of Aberdeen,
" and by this my preſent charter, to
" found, gift, and perpetually mortify to
" them, all and haill the Place or Monaſ-
" tery of the Holy Trinity of the brethren
" of the burgh of Aberdeen, &c."—to be
" an hoſpital for the *poor old Tradeſmen* of
" the ſaid burgh, to be ſuſtained in the
" ſame, who ſhall be of *good fame*, and not
" *redacted to poverty through their own vice,*
" *or drunkenneſs and intemperance;* and there-
" fore that none be brought into the ſaid
" hoſpital, or *receive of the fruits of the ſaid*
" *mortification*, but *good, holy, and ſober men.*"

Particular directions are given, in regard
to the powers of the Patron, the mode of
admitting to the benefit of this eſtabliſh-
ment,

ment, the office of Mafter of the hofpital, the internal economy of the houfe, and the behaviour of its inhabitants. In fome articles, time and circumftances have rendered alterations neceffary ; but the great object of the founder has been always kept in view, and the produce of the fund uniformly devoted to the relief of thofe, for whom it was originally intended.

It is indeed, but juftice to the Corporations of Aberdeen, in their prefent Patron, here to fay, after he has repeatedly examined their accounts, that he has found much reafon to approve, and that he is not acquainted with any funds, which are more impartially, more economically, or in any refpect better managed than theirs.

The Trades Hofpital had enjoyed, but a fhort while, the prefiding care of its founder, when he was called to the exer-

cife

cife of his virtue, in another way. It was the lot of this good man, to live in times of much public commotion, and to pafs through fcenes of more than common difficulty and peril. He had occafion to witnefs great national contefts, in which they, who had long been friends and neighbours, were lamentably divided, and inflamed with mutual rancour and animofity. Nor could he, however moderate in his principles, however inoffenfive in his conduct, efcape the hardfhips to which, in fuch a ftate of things, he was inevitably expofed.

The baneful feeds of national difcontent had been fown in Scotland, when King *James* attempted to eftablifh there, the forms and ceremonies of the Englifh Church. Though his Majefty defifted, from urging the fcheme of a complete conformity, he prevailed upon the Affembly,

bly, held at *Perth* in the year 1618, to admit some parts of the English Ritual. [c]

But these *Articles of Perth*, as they were afterwards called, were so little regarded by the clergy, and so disagreeable to the people in general, that, immediately on King *Charles'* accession to the throne, an application was made to him, requesting that he would dispense with their being observed. The Scotch Bishops themselves, were so sensible of the necessity of forbearance in this matter, that they had not pressed the observance of the offensive articles, or had connived at the neglect of them: Never indeed were moderate and conciliatory measures more necessary, than at this critical period. But unfortunately *Charles* had not, among his counsellors, a Bishop *Andrews*.

The person, whose opinion had most

weight

weight with him, at leaft in ecclefiaftical matters, was Archbifhop *Laud;* a man of acknowledged probity and learning, but intemperately zealous for pomp and ceremony, in divine fervice. Hence, he encouraged the king, to proceed in thofe meafures, refpecting the Church of Scotland, which the more cautious Prelate, whom *James* had confulted, perfuaded that Prince to abandon. Steps were accordingly taken, which many of the Scots confidered as encroachments, both on their religious and their civil rights. Murmurs, complaints, remonftrances, and at laft, infurrections enfued.

The firft popular commotion of any magnitude took place at *Edinburgh* (23 July 1637) when an attempt was made there to introduce the *Liturgy*, which his Majefty, by proclamation, had appointed

to

to be ufed, in the public worfhip of the
Church of Scotland. Religion and liberty,
things too precious and important to be
rafhly touched, were now thought to be in
danger. In fuch a caufe, zeal is certainly
laudable, while it maintains its proper
character, and moves in a due concurrence
with knowledge. But, it is fometimes apt
to ftep out of courfe; to be clamorous and
violent; and, in its eagernefs for the end,
not to be very fcrupulous about the means.
It was thus, with the populace of Edinburgh, in oppofing the Liturgy; a form
of worfhip, with which they were entirely
unacquainted, and which they confidered
as needlefs and inexpedient, if not finful.

The prejudices of the mob were, perhaps, fomented by the lurking emiffaries
of faction. But, there was foon an oppofition, of a more fteady and deliberate
kind.

kind, countenanced and fupported by men of real patriotifm, and who were actuated by motives not unworthy of the caufe.

At this alarming crifis, when the refentment and jealoufy of the nation were aroufed, it was thought neceffary to eftablifh, as a teft of principle, that famous *Covenant*, which has been fo much applauded by fomé, and fo much reprobated by others. Impartially confidered, it was little more than a folemn renunciation of Popery, and a mutual bond, by which the fubfcribers engaged, upon oath, to oppofe all religious innovations, and to affift each other againft all their enemies. As its tenour was perfectly agreeable to the general fentiments of the nation, this engagement was, in a fhort time, voluntarily fubfcribed by perfons of all ranks and conditions.

Among

Among thofe who refufed to concur, there were none who fo honourably dif- tinguifhed themfelves as the Clergy of Aberdeen, and the Profeffors of King's and Marifchal Colleges. But thefe reverend and learned men, being influenced by prin- ciples, more noble and generous than thofe of party, were no fooner fatisfied that the meafure was, in itfelf, lawful and right, than they readily give it their fupport. Moft of them, it is known, came at laft to fubfcribe the Covenant; and the few, who perfifted in refufing, craved only an indul- gence to their fcruples, which was not un- reafonable, but which the public mind was then too violently agitated to allow.

Subfcription to the Covenant was not, however, fo rigoroufly enforced, as to pro- hibit all exercife of private judgment. Doctor Guild, and Mr. Robert Reid, Minifter at Banchory-ternan, were permitted to fubfcribe it, under fuch limitations, as they themfelves were pleafed to fpecify. Others were, no doubt, admitted to the fame privilege, though the fact cannot now be fo clearly afcertained. With refpect to Dr. Guild and Mr. Reid, it is indifputable. An authentic copy of the certificate which they received from the Marquis of Montrofe, the Lord Couper, the Mafter of Forbes, Sir Thomas Burnett of Leys, — Laird of Morphie, Mr. Alexander Henderfon, Minifter at Leuchars in Fife, Mr. David Dickfon, Minifter at Irvine, and Mr. Andrew Cant, Minifter at Pitfligo, as Commiffioners from the Covenanters, is tranfmitted to pofterity, and is expreffed in the following terms.

" Doctor William Guild and Mr Robert " Reid have fubfcribed the Covenant made

E. " by

" by the Noblemen, Barons, Gentry, and
" Minifters, anent the maintenance of re-
" ligion, his Majefty's authority and laws,
" with thefe exprefs *Conditions*, to wit;
" That we acknowledge not, nor yet con-
" demn, the Articles of Perth, to be un-
" lawful or heads of Popery, but only pro-
" mife (for the peace of the church, and
" other reafons) to forbear the practice
" thereof for a time.

" *Secondly*, That we condemn not epif-
" copal government, fecluding the perfo-
" nal abufe thereof.

" *Thirdly*, That we ftill retain, and fhall
" retain, all loyal and dutiful fubjection
" and obedience, unto our dread Sove-
" reign the King's Majefty; And that in
" this fenfe, and no otherwife, we have
" put our hands to the forefaid Covenant,
" thefe Noblemen, Barons, and Minifters,
                                        " com-

" commiffioners, under fubfcribing, do tef-
" tify, at Aberdeen, the 30th of July 1638.

(figned) " *William Guild.*

" *Robert Reid.*"

" Likeas we, under fubfcribers, do de-
" clare, that they neither had, nor have,
" any intention but of loyalty to his Ma-
" jefty, as the faid Covenant bears.

(figned) " *Montrofe.*

" *Couper, &c.*"

About two months after this, Dr. Guild
was appointed by the Prefbytery of Aberdeen, to be one of their Commiffioners to
the General Affembly, which was to meet
at Glafgow, on the twenty firft of November following; a diftinction, at that period,
more honourable than fafe, to thofe who
received it. Some of the Commiffioners
did not attend; but no private confidera-
tion could induce Dr. Guild, to fhrink

from

from a public duty, which it was then of the greateft importance refolutely to difcharge. He repaired therefore to Glafgow in due time; was prefent in that memorable Affembly, which abolifhed the Hierarchy of the church of Scotland; and conducted himfelf on the occafion, as became an enlightened and Chriftian Divine. The other Commiffioners from Aberdeen, who gave attendance, were *Mr. David Lindfay*, Minifter of Belhelvie, and *Mr. John Lundie*, Profeffor of Humanity in King's College.

It is probable, from the limitations under which he fubfcribed the Covenant, that Dr. Guild was inclined to favour Epifcopacy; but his endeavours in the caufe were directed, by that difcretion, which governs zeal, and tempers refolution. Fervent without enthufiafm, he was

more

more zealous for the effentials of religion, than for its appendages; and, however much he might regret the falling Hierarchy, he was defirous, **by** prudent conceffions, *to keep the* **unity** *of the Spirit in the bond of peace.* Such were the principles upon which he feems to have acted, **in** the important commiffion, **with** which he **was** then intrufted.

After his return from Glafgow, he officiated, as formerly, with his colleagues at Aberdeen, in the paftoral function. Jointly endeavouring to do good to the people among whom they miniftered, they **had** perhaps no thought of being feparated, when **they** were obliged fuddenly to defift from their ufual labours, **and** to leave the place where they had been fo ufefully employed. His colleagues went to England; and **Dr. Guild** withdrew to Holland, where

E 3   he

he would certainly have remained much
longer than he did, had his choice been
determined, by what was moft for his
own comfort and tranquillity. Another
very different principle, a refolution to
fhare in the trials and fufferings of his op-
preffed countrymen, brought him back to
Aberdeen in a few months. Doctor Sibbald alfo returned, about the fame time,
and with the fame magnanimous refolution.
They were both received, with a readi-
nefs fomewhat encouraging, and immediately invited to refume the exercife of their
miniftry; but their profpect was, in other
refpects, as dark and comfortlefs as ever.
The angry paffions of men were now ex-
ceedingly inflamed; the difficulties, dif-
treffes, and dangers of the country, mul-
tiplied; and all things concurring to fill
the

the confiderate mind, with melancholy forebodings of national mifery.

Dr. Guild, like a true patriot, was anxious to heal thofe diffentions, which had been fo unwarily excited, and which fome recent events had unhappily ferved to exafperate. With this view, when the Covenant had received the fanction of his Majefty and the Privy Council, he endeavoured, in a pious and affectionate Addrefs to the Public, to diffufe a fpirit of religious and loyal attention to the fubject, which no good man of any party could condemn.

This performance was entitled, " *A* " *friendly and faithful Advice to the Nobility,* " *Gentry and others ;*" and it was not unworthy of the name. Even thofe, who differed widely in political fentiments, concurred in acknowledging, that it advifed well. The ftyle of it, however exceptionable in

E 4   fome

some respects, will not appear despicable, when compared with that of contemporary writers; and to compare it with the style of others would be unfair. In regard to the subject, though it may be thought by some, to favour of the doctrine of passive obedience and non-resistance, others will be of opinion, that it contains many things, no less favourable to the liberties of the people, than to the prerogative of the prince.

It was the misfortune of that age, to experience the miseries of a contest, in which there was too great forgetfulness of both; and to exemplify, in the most awful manner, the fatal consequences of encroachment, whether regal or popular. As a warning against the cause of these formidable evils, the *advice* of Dr. Guild might have been of essential service to his country,

try, had it been but as faithfully applied, as it was wifely given. The friends of royalty, would not then have foftered in the prince, thofe lofty ideas of prerogative, which were above all control, and which prompted him to the hated meafures, fo fatal to his peace. Nor would the oppofers of arbitrary domination, have withheld from him that due refpect and obedience, which the order of fociety requires, and without which the ends of government cannot be obtained. He himfelf would have renounced every defire to govern, without the concurrence of his fubjects; would have been tender of their rights; and defirous of their friendfhip, as well as of their obedience. All would have check-ed their encroaching, injurious, and refent-ful paffions, and cordially united, in exer-

ting

ting their beft endeavours for the public good. [D]

The moft refpectable perfon, who per-fifted in refufing to fubfcribe the Covenant, when it was tendered by **royal** authority at Aberdeen, was the reverend Dr. William Leflie, Principal of King's College. A for-feiture **of his** office, which many friendly endeavours had been ufed to prevent, was the confequence: for fubfcription to the *Confeffion* and *Covenant* was now required by act of parliament, *under all civil pains.* [E]

Under the unpleafing neceffity of de-priving Dr. Leflie, a much efteemed and amiable man, the members of King's Col-lege, to whom the choice of a Principal belonged, had fome confolation in the character and merit of the perfons, who were propofed to fucceed him.

Doctor William Guild, and Mr. Robert
Baillie,

Baillie, another clergyman of very high repute, were feverally recommended to the electors; who, on the eighteenth of Auguft 1640, decided in favour of Dr. Guild.

Honoured as he was, by this preference, Dr. Guild feems to have accepted the office of Principal, rather in compliance with the wifhes of others, than to gratify any defire of his own. It was not till long after his election, that he confented to the appointment of a day for his admiffion, and formally refigned his minifterial charge. He preached for the laft time, as Minifter of Aberdeen, on the twenty feventh of June 1641. But, though his paftoral relation to his native city then ceafed, his affection and good offices to its inhabitants were continued all his life.

Of his undiminifhed zeal for their fpi-
ritual

ritual interefts he had occafion once to give
them, what feemed at the time, a very
hazardous proof.   After the Marquis of
Montrofe had defeated the Covenanters,
(September the 13th, 1644) in a bloody
battle, which he continued, from the place
where it commenced, about two miles
weft, even to the ftreets of Aberdeen ; the
citizens fuffered fo much from the favage
cruelty of his foldiers, that they dreaded
the return of fuch ferocious vifiters.   On
the news, therefore, of his approach a fecond time, almoft all the inhabitants of
Aberdeen were filled with terror and dif-
may.   Thofe who thought themfelves moft
obnoxious, among whom were the Clergy,
left their habitations and fled.   Dr. Guild,
it may be fuppofed, was not without his
apprehenfions of the danger, but he remained at his poft ; and, in the abfence of
their

their ordinary paftors, regularly preached to his late parifhioners, the people of Aberdeen.

His fucceffor, in the minifterial office, at Aberdeen, appears to have been the not a little famed Mr. *Andrew Cant;* one of the moft popular preachers of the age, and the perfon from whom, it is faid, the *Spectator* derived the word to *cant;* but Andrew, as one remarks, " canted, in all probability, " no more than others of his time ;" and a more natural derivation of the word may be very eafily conceived.

In whatever ftation of life a man is placed, his character muft depend on the correfpondence between his behaviour, and that which his fituation requires. At the head of a fociety, whofe important object was the education of youth, no one was ever more defervedly refpected than Dr. Guild.

Guild. Inſtructed, cheriſhed, and encouraged by him, genius was called forth into
exertion, and modeſt merit was excited to
diſtinguiſh itſelf. To ſkill and induſtry,
in promoting the literary progreſs of his
pupils, he added the moſt zealous and un-
wearied endeavours, to form in their hearts
thoſe ſentiments of virtue, and to confirm
them in thoſe ſacred principles of religion,
without which all human ſcience is of little uſe.

His Sovereign King *Charles I*, in the
midſt of the troubles which diſturbed his
reign, gave all the encouragement in his
power to learning and learned men.
King's College, Aberdeen, was honoured
with more than an ordinary ſhare of the
royal favour; and received (1641) in con-
junction with Mariſchal College, the name
of the *Caroline Univerſity*. [r] The particular

cular merit of the worthy Principal, did not escape the notice of his Majesty, who bestowed upon Dr. Guild, *a free gift of the house and garden, which had formerly been the residence of the Bishop of Aberdeen.* Such a mark of royal approbation, could not have been conferred more properly. It was a commendable tribute of respect, to generally acknowledged worth; and, in every view, must have been very acceptable to Dr. Guild. He did not however allow it to increase his private fortune; for, with that generosity and beneficence, for which he was so remarkable, he devoted this present to the service of the public. The College, the town, and the poor of the parish of Old Machar, derived from it each some additional accommodation.

But how various and uncertain are human events, and how little under the con-

troul

troul of wifdom and virtue! While Dr. Guild was fo munificently exerting himfelf, for the good of future generations, as well as of the age in which he lived, who could have thought that, inftead of efteem and gratitude, he was foon to meet with infult and oppreffion! Even amidft the violence of contending parties, fome tendernefs might have been expected, towards a man of fuch eminent virtue. But the malignant perfecuting fpirit of party fuppreffes every generous fentiment, remembers no obligations, and extinguifhes even the fympathetic feelings of humanity.

The difturbances which had commenced in Scotland, having in a fhort time fpread to England, the flame of civil war was kindled, in all parts of the Britifh Empire. Nor was it extinguifhed, without occafion-

ing

ing the tragical death of the King, and the subverfion of the Monarchy.

As Dr. **Guild** was probably fufpected of too **ftrong an** attachment to the royal caufe, he incurred the difpleafure of the ruling powers. Commiffioners were appointed to vifit King's College, by whofe authority the Principal, the Sub-principal, and two of the profeffors, were depofed. But as this fentence was extremely difagreeable to the Univerfity, the gentlemen upon whom it was paffed, were immediately reinftated, or rather were not difplaced.

Dr. Guild held the office of Principal about two years longer, till he was depofed, in the year 1651, by five commiffioners of a very imperious kind (Fenwick, Molfey, Owen, Defborough, and Smith) *Colonels* from the army of *General Monk ;* gentlemen very well qualified, perhaps, to have

F   been

been members of a Court Martial, but apparently not fo fit to have been Vifitors of an Univerfity. They left, however, the election of another Principal, to the proper judges; and the office was beftowed (1652) upon Mr. *John Row*, one of the Minifters of Aberdeen.

Mr Row had been early patronifed, by the Lord Chancellor Hay, of Kinnoul; and had acquired confiderable reputation, as Rector of an academy at *Perth*. He publifhed fome very ufeful tracts, particularly a Grammar and Vocabulary of the Hebrew language; and was juftly accounted a man of learning and abilities. Prefixed to his grammar we find, the unanimous approbation of the Faculty of the College of St. Leonard, in the Univerfity of St. Andrews; and very ample teftimonies to the merit of the author, from

Mr.

Mr. Alexander Henderfon, Mr. Samuel Rutherford, and other refpectable individuals. To excel in oriental literature, at leaft in a knowledge of Hebrew, was in Mr. Row a kind of family inheritance. His grandfather, Dr. John Row, is faid to have been the firft, who publicly taught Hebrew, in Scotland. He was a man of fome eminence in the church of Rome, and had been fent into Scotland by the Pope, in the beginning of the Reformation, with ample authority to oppofe and check the progrefs of the reformed religion. But, being converted from Popery by the celebrated reformer *John Knox*, he renounced the errors of the Romifh faith, and became *Superintendent* of the reformed church at Perth; in which fituation he lived to a great age, much refpected and efteemed. His fon, the father of Principal Row, had

F 2

difcover-

difcovered fome genius for Hebrew, when he was only a child of four or five years old.

The vacancy at Aberdeen, in confequence of the removal of Mr. Row to King's College, put it now in the power of the Prefbytery, to have replaced Dr. Guild in his paftoral charge, which he had not refigned, but in fubmiffion to their authority. He was ftill able for its labours, and defirous of being reftored to his miniftry; and, for this he applied to the Prefbytery, on the fixth of April 1652; but in vain. Several members of the Prefbytery, it is thought, were heartily inclined to have granted his requeft; but after fome delay, a majority concurred, not indeed in rejecting, but in continuing his petition before them, *that the Prefbytery might think more maturely thereon.* He appealed

pealed to the Synod; but that his appeal was ever argued or heard by that **venerable court**, is not certain; it is too **certain**, that the object of it **was** never obtained.

There are times, when " the post of " honour is a private station." If it was not now the post of honour, it was at least not inglorious to Dr. Guild. He, though divested of office, was still dignified in character; still distinguished, as an ancient philosopher (Pythagoras) said the **man** should be, who has the nearest resemblance to celestial beings, by *beneficence and truth*. Living retired, however, and praying for the peace of his distressed country,

" Content he was to be obscurely good."

As Aberdeen became his place of residence, for the remainder of his life, the Incorporated Trades had again the honour

of

of his perfonal prefence and affiftance, as
their Patron. His liberal mind was ever
devifing liberal things. Of this, another
remarkable proof is a legacy to the Corporations, which is mentioned, as follows,
in the record of his bequefts, September
15, 1655: " —That out of the charitable
" difpofition he had to the poor, and in
" obedience to the Lord's precepts, 1 *Tim,*
" vi. 17. and *Heb.* xiii. 16. he bound and
" obliged him, and his heirs allenarly, to
" the Mafter of Hofpital, Deacon Conve-
" ner of the Crafts of Aberdeen for the
" time, and remanent Deacons, to pay to
" them, the fum of *Five Thoufand Merks*
" Scots money, at the next term after his
" deceafe, for the entertaining of three
" poor boys who are craftfmens fons, as
" Burfars in the New College of Aberdeen,
" who are of good engynes, and able for
                                        " the

" the faid College, and either have not pa-
" rents to put them to the College, **or**
" whofe parents are poor, and known **to**
" be unable to maintain them thereat ;
" but if it fhould pleafe his heirs rather to
" denude themfelves of the heritable right,
" which he had of his forehoufe in the
" Caftlegate, wherein he himfelf dwelt,
" and brew-houfe (or victual houfe) with
" the room above, on the other **fide of the**
" clofe, rather than to **pay** the five thou-
" fand merks, in that cafe, he bound and
" obliged his heirs, to denude themfelves
" of the heritable right of the faid houfe,
" in favour of the Trades, for the ufe fore-
" named, the infeftment to be on the ex-
" pence of the Mortifier of the Trinity
" Hofpital, referving to the Mortifier's
" wife her life-rent of the houfe.——If any
" variance fhould be, concerning the be-

" flowing

" ftowing of any of thefe burfes, the eldeft
" Minifter of Aberdeen (as the moft con-
" fcientious to fee mortifications go right)
" to decide therein.——And that impartially
" the faid benefit be beftowed, out of the
" rents of the houfe, upon the unableft in
" means, and beft qualified in gifts, as they
" fhall anfwer to God——which houfe in all
" time coming (that it, nor the rents there-
" of, be not perverted to any other ufe)
" to be called *the Burfars' houfe;* and when
" any of them are laureat, they by writing
" to oblige themfelves, for the benefit re-
" ceived, when God enables them, to add
" to this mortification; and this their
" writing to be carefully kept in the Maf-
" ter of Hofpital's box, either by itfelf, or
" rather in a book made for the purpofe,
" who (the Mafter of Hofpital) fhall fet the
" houfe, by advice of the Convener and
                 " Deacons,

" Deacons, and uptake the rents thereof,
" and be conjunct with them, in the pa-
" tronage and election of said bursars."

The heirs of Dr. Guild chose rather to give the house, than to pay the money; and it has ever since been managed, under the name of *The Bursars' house*, by the Master of the Trinity Hospital, and the other trustees, for the support of bursars at Marischal College.

There is a tradition, that Dr. Guild received a grant of this house, and some other property, from King *Charles the II*; in return for *a bason full of gold*, which the Doctor presented to his Majesty, when he came to Aberdeen. But though the King, who at that time (*March* 1652) stood very much in need of pecuniary aid, may have received from Dr. Guild such a mark of attachment, it was not then in his power

as

as Sovereign to have made any grant effectual. It has indeed been said, that he was always more liberal in good words and promises, than in substantial testimonies of his gratitude. How generous, or how grateful, if he was under the alleged obligation, he would have been to Dr. Guild, can only be conjectured, as that dutiful subject did not live to see the Restoration.

During his retirement, Dr. Guild added to the number of his theological works, *An Explication and Application of the Song of Solomon*, dedicated to the right honourable, the *Provost, Magistrates*, and *Council* of *Edinburgh*.—The *Sealed Book opened*, or an explanation of the Revelation of St. John. *An Answer to a Popish Pamphlet*, called *The Touchstone of the Reformed Gospel, made specially out of themselves*, dedicated to *Sir Thomas Mudie*, Provost, and the other Magistrates ftrates of *Dundee*—The *Novelty of Popery discovered, and chiefly proven by Romanists out of themselves*, dedicated to the worfhipful, and worthy of all refpect, *David Wilkie, Dean of Guild of Edinburgh.*

He is alfo faid to have been the author of an effay, entitled, *An Antidote against Popery;* but of this, there is only prefumptive evidence. The other performances here afcribed to him, though fome of them are not now to be found, are all known to have been written, and publifhed by him. Moft of them are enumerated, in a letter, from the celebrated grammarian and antiquary, *Mr. Thomas Ruddiman,* to a learned friend, as in Mr. Ruddiman's library; and a few of them, as reprinted under his infpection. That letter was obligingly communicated to the author of this inquiry, by Mr. Ruddiman's correfpondent; and

it

it contains, as fhall appear afterwards, very favourable fentiments of Dr. Guild, and his writings.

The life of Dr. Guild, fuitably to its beneficent progrefs, terminated with acts of charity. By his laft will, which was written in the year 1657, a fhort while before he died, he bequeathed feven thoufand merks, " to be fecured on land, by " the Town-council and Kirk-feffion of " Aberdeen, the yearly profit of which to " be applied, for the fuftentation of poor " orphans, to hold them at fchools or trades, " impartially, without inverting any way " this mortification, as they fhall anfwer " to God." Nor was he unmindful of the poor, among his firft, and ever-affectionate flock, at King-Edward; but devoted alfo to them, a proportion of his public bounty. The Univerfity of St. Andrews, much indebted,

debted, in other refpects, to his liberal patronage, received a legacy of his library;
excepting only one valuable manufcript,
fuppofed by fome to be the original or
firft copy, of the memorable *Letter* from the
States of Bohemia and *Moravia*, to the *Council
of Conftance* (1415) relative to *John Hufs* and
Jerome of Prague, which he bequeathed to
the Univerfity of Edinburgh. [G]

A defcription of this manufcript, and a
detail of what it contains, may be found, by
thofe who wifh for further information
concerning it, in Maitland's Hiftory of
Edinburgh. According to that author,
who feems to have examined it very mi-
nutely, there is reafon to think, that it is
an original. He introduces it to the notice
of his readers (B. VI. p. 371.) as a very
great curiofity; and traces its progrefs, to
the place where it now is, thus—" brought
" to

" to *Scotland* by a gentleman, at his return
" from his travels in foreign parts, probably
" about one hundred years ago; for by
" *Comenius* it appears to have been in the
" College library of *Aberdeen* above eighty
" feven years fince; but, that it did not
" belong to that library, is manifeft by
" Dr. *William Guild's* having bequeathed
" the fame to the College of *Edinburgh* in
" the year 1657; and it being received by
" the Town-council in the month of *Ja-*
" *nuary*, *Anno* 1658, they ordered a receipt
" to be given to his relict *Katharine Rolland*
" for the fame."

Bequefts and donations equally numerous, and equally judicious, with thofe
which are on record of Dr. Guild, have
been given by few. But fo great an abi-
lity to do good, fo ftrong an inclination,
and fo enlarged an underftanding to direct
them

them, as he poffeffed, do not often meet in one perfon.

Mrs Guild, who feems to have refembled her hufband much, in the benevolent affections of her mind, followed his example, in the charitable deeds of her life. In a Latin oration in praife of the benefactors of Marifchal College, publifhed in the year 1702, while the Orator (Mr. William Smith) makes honourable mention of Doctor Guild, and calls him " a moft reli- " gious man, of profound learning, unfpot- " ted holinefs, and eminent piety," he com- pares him to *Zacharias*, and his wife to *Elifabeth*—" The glory," fays he, " of her " age and fex, for virtue and piety, and her " vaft donations. For, by her munifi- " cence, are maintained fix ftudents of " philofophy, four fcholars at the public " fchool, two ftudents of divinity, fix poor widows,

" widows, and as many poor men's chil-
" dren.   Had fhe lived in other times, and
" in another country, fhe had undoubtedly
" been canonized as a faint."

She did not long furvive her beloved
hufband.   But before fhe died, a Monu-
ment was, at her expence, erected to his
memory (1659) in the church-yard of St.
Nicholas in Aberdeen; on the principal
tablet of which, is the following infcription.

SANCTISS. ET INDIVID. TRINITATI

S.

ET PIÆ MEMORIÆ GULIELMI GUILD,

QUI IN HAC URBE NATUS ET INSTITUTUS,

SACRISQUE STUDIIS A TENERIS INNUTRITUS,

PRIMUM CURÆ ECCLESIÆ DE KINEDWARD ADMOTUS,

EAQUE PER XXIII ANNOS ADMINISTRATA,

A MUNICIPIBUS SUIS IN HANC URBEM VOCATUS,

JAM SS. THEOLOGIÆ D. ET CAROLO REGI A SACRIS,

PER DECENNIUM HIC ECCLESIASTIS MUNERE FUNCTUS;

UNDE TRANSLATUS AD COLLEGIUM REGALE,

UBI PRIMARII ONUS AD DECENNIUM SUSTINUIT;

DONEC REBUS APUD NOS TURBATIS,

INTEGRITAS EJUS LIVOREM TEMPORUM NON EFFUGIT;

INDE IGITUR DIGRESSUS,

HIC, UBI CUNABULA, NIDUM SENECTUTIS POSUIT:

NON TAMEN INERTI OTIO DEDITUS,

SED VOCE, CALAMO, ET INCULPATA VITA,

ALIIS EXEMPLO FUIT.

AMPLUM ET INNOCENTER PARTUM PATRIMONIUM,

MULTO MAXIMAM PARTEM PIIS USIBUS LEGAVIT.

CONJUNX QUOQUE,

QUÆ SUA ERANT IISDEM USIBUS ADDIXIT.

VIXIT ANNOS LXXI,

ET

AD VII KALENDAS AUGUSTI, ANNI MDCLVII,

IN SPEM OPTATISSIMÆ RESURRECTIONIS,

MORTALITATEM EXPLEVIT.

KATHARINA ROWEN, SUPERSTES VIDUA,

DILECTISS. MARITO,

CUM QUO CONCORDITER XLVII PLENOS ANNOS VIXIT,

H. M. L. M. F. C.

NEC CÆPISSE, NEC FECISSE VIRTUTIS EST,

SED PERFECISSE.

G   Such

Such is the account, which authentic records warrant us to give, of the life of Doctor Guild; in whom were conspicuous, not only the talents of a man truly great, but the ftill more eftimable qualities of one eminently good. For, capacity and genius derive their value, only from their ufe.

The real character, it has been faid, is moft clearly feen, when one is placed in circumftances, not of tranquillity, but of commotion and trouble. But in times of fuch national ferment, as thofe in which Dr. Guild lived, Hiftorians do not always fpeak of public tranfactions with impartiality, nor delineate public characters with candour. On the contrary, men of all defcriptions are then praifed or cenfured, not in proportion to their deferts, but according to their political principles and

con-

connexions. Hence, the invectives of a certain writer (the only one indeed who mentions him difrefpectfully) againft the man of whofe real excellence we have found, in tracing his actions, fo many inconteftable proofs.

The name of this partial Hiftorian, if he can be called an *Hiftorian*, is *John Spalding ;* whofe " Journal of the Troubles and Me- " morable Tranfactions in Scotland, from " 1624 to 1645," tho' long confined, in manufcript, to the libraries of a few, has been lately printed, and publifhed. As he was contemporary with Dr. Guild, his invidious remarks upon the conduct of that venerable man, feemed to require fome antidote, and partly occafioned the Inquiry into facts and circumftances, of which a detail is given in the preceding pages.

His attacks upon Dr. Guild are various,

and

and violent; but there is no part of the
Doctor's conduct, which seems to have
given more unpardonable offence to Spalding, than his devoting the old materials
of the Bishop's house, dove-coat, and garden walls, to purposes which this angry
writer deemed profane. He speaks of it
repeatedly, in the most indignant terms.
" The baillies of Old Aberdeen," says he,
(vol. 1. page 336.) " John Forbes and
" Thomas Mercer, by tolerance of Dr.
" Guild Principal, caused masons throw
" down to the ground the Bishop's dove-
" coat (whilk indeed was ruinous and un-
" profitable) to be stones to the bigging of
" a Song-school, whilk by some was not
" thought sacrilegious, but yet was evil
" done, as others thought."

" In the same manner, (vol 2. p. 27.)
" he (Dr. Guild) dang down the walls of
                                    " the

" the Snow-kirk, to big the College dykes."
—" Now he is demolifhing the Bifhop's
" houfe, pitiful and lamentable to behold;
" kirks and ftately buildings firft caften
" down by ruffians and rafcals, and next
" by churchmen, under colour of religion."

In this volume alfo (p. 43, 44.) he adds,
" Dr. Guild, at his own hand, caufed
" brake down the great oaken joifts, with-
" in the Bifhop's houfe, and tranfported
" them therefrae, for reparation of the
" College. Pitiful to fee fo glorious a
" building thus thrown down by defpiteful
" Soldiers, and then demolifhed by Doctors
" of Divinity.

And again, (p. 127.) " Dr. Guild goes
" on moft malicioufly, and caufes caft
" down the ftately wall ftanding within
" the Bifhop's clofe, curioufly builded with
" hewn ftone, and took the ftones down

G 3

" to

" to the College, for fuch vain ufes as he
" thought moft expedient (fuch was the
" iniquity of the times) and brake down
" the afhlar work about the turrets, raifed
" the pavement of the hall, and caufed
" lead them down, to lay the floor of the
" common fchool."

Yet, after all this vehement outcry,
Spalding is not afhamed to acknowledge,
that fome of thefe *glorious* buildings were
indeed ruinous and unprofitable; and that
what he had cenfured, with fo much acri-
mony, as a kind of facrilege, was only an
application of Doctor Guild's own property
to public purpofes, which happened unfortunately not to be fuch as Mr. Spalding
would have been pleafed to recommend.
" It is true," fays he, (vol. 2. p. 262.) " this
" houfe, yards, and precincts, were given
" to him by the Eftates, whereof he might
            " have

" have made *a more godly ufe*, by upholding
" rather than demolifhing the fame."

To the intelligent reader, thefe fpecimens
of Spalding's Journal will be fufficient.
In them he will clearly difcern the difpofition of that author towards Dr. Guild,
and will draw the unavoidable inference.

Againft fuch railing, a formal vindication
of the Doctor's character is not intended,
and cannot be neceffary. A narrative of
his life has been given, confirmed by evidence about which there can be no difpute;
and what better anfwer can there be, to
the cenfures of ignorance, or the calumnies of envy, than a plain account of the
truth? Had fuch fatisfaction been unattain-
able, in the cafe before us; yet the general
character of Mr. Spalding, as an author,
might have rendered an attack from him,
of little confequence. It is drawn thus

G 4 (not

(not a very amiable picture) though by a
friendly hand; " The public tranfactions,
" of which Spalding gives an account, are
" greatly mifreprefented.—Spalding was a
" Royalift, but fpeaks with great candour
" of the oppofite party, and with particu-
" lar refpect of fome Covenanting Mini-
" fters, whom he extols as good preachers.
" But of *Mr. Andrew Cant*, and the *Pref-*
" *byterian Clergy* in general, he loves to
" tell every prejudice he can. The ftyle
" is vulgar, but has merit†."

His defects of ftyle would have been
eafily pardoned, had the fubftance of his
performance been of value: Had he thrown
any new light, upon public tranfactions;
made any difcoveries, in the fecret views
of parties: eftablifhed any certainty, with
regard to the real characters of particular

† Bibliotheca Topograph. Britan.

perfons;

perfons : and rendered undeviating juftice
to all. But inftead of this, we find in
Spalding, a virulent party writer ; endeavouring as much as poffible, on every occafion, to defame and vilify thofe, whofe
political or religious fentiments happened
to differ from his ; and not a little defec-
tive in that veracity, which is the firft
virtue of the Hiftorian. There is, in what
he fays of Dr. Guild alone, fuch a palpable
want of candour, as cannot fail to difguft
difcerning readers ; and fuch opprobrious
railing, as fome have long ago indignantly
cenfured.

Mr. Ruddiman, in the letter already
mentioned, tells his friend, " I have been,
" for upwards of forty years paft, picking
" up fuch of Doctor Guild's works, as I
" could light on ; from the great efteem I
" had always conceived of that excellent
" divine.

" divine.—And I would be content to
" know, what it was that moved the fpleen
" of Spalding againft Dr. Guild, which
" made him give fuch an unfavourable re-
" prefentation of the actions of that great
" man ; whether it proceeded from a pri-
" vate grudge, or from the part that author
" took in the civil commotions of thofe
" times."

Befides what he fays of Dr. Guild, and
his writings, in general ; Mr. Ruddiman
expreffes himfelf more particularly, and in
very ftrong terms, as to the peculiar merit
of fome of the Doctor's performances ;
and, if an opinion may be formed of the
reft, from thofe now extant, they were all
of them works, if not of brilliant genius,
yet of found fenfe, theological knowledge,
and rational piety.

The opponent of Mr. Ruddiman as a
Gram-

Grammarian, *Mr. James Man*, agreed entirely with him in his cenfure of Spalding. "By his account of Dr. Guild," fays he, "it appears that Spalding has been a man "of no great genius, fince he defcends to "fuch low and trivial things, and makes "much ado about nothing."

Not to multiply teftimonies in favour of Doctor Guild, I fhall only add that of a writer, who had certainly accefs to the moft accurate information concerning his character, if he had not a perfonal acquaintance with him. It is given, in the *Appendix* to *Spotifwood's Hiftory* of the Church of Scotland, when the author fpeaks of the depofition of Principal Leflie. "In "his room," fays he, "was elected *William* "*Guild*, Doctor of Divinity, Minifter in "Aberdeen, and one of the Chaplains to "King Charles the firft, *a learned and wor-*

"*thy*

" *thy person.*" Though that publication .was anonymous, I have now before me .proof, that the author of it was *a Clergyman* of *Canterbury*, two of whose neareſt relations were Profeſſors in King's College, .while Doctor Guild was Principal.

The approbation of men of knowledge and abilities, which was ſo liberally beſtowed on Dr. Guild, is a ſufficient indication of true merit; but very uncommon excellence is neceſſary to command and ſecure the general eſteem. The light muſt be very clear, where the dimmeſt eye perceives it; and the conviction very ſtrong, where every man of plain ſenſe, as well as the man of more diſcernment, feels its force. Yet, of the general eſtimation, in which Dr. Guild and his writings were held, it is at leaſt a preſumptive proof, that after his death, in the year 1658, a collection

lection of his works was *reprinted* at London. Bookſellers do not uſually pay this compliment to works, for which there is little demand.

But, the Journal of Spalding, though injurious enough to Dr. Guild as a writer, goes ſtill further than to deprive him of literary merit. It aims at his reputation a more miſchievous thruſt, and repreſents him as a man of very flexible and temporizing principles. How degrading the character, and how unjuſt! Doctor Guild maintained his principles with exemplary firmneſs, though not with bigotry; he was ſteady, but not dogmatical; and if, at any time, he varied his opinions, it was according to the views he received of truth. What but this, which has been the conduct of all wiſe and honeſt men, was to be expected

pected from Dr. Guild? The intolerant
Zealot is ever obstinate, and shuts his eyes
against the light; the Slave of Party will
not admit a ray, which would discover
truths opposing his prejudices and passions:
but the Man of Candour and Honesty is
desirous of light and knowledge, will ever
make Truth his guide, and will follow her
whithersoever she leads him.

To say more, in regard to the aspersions
of Spalding, would perhaps be superfluous;
to have said less, would have been some-
thing worse. It would have been iniqui-
tous, in the Memorialist of Dr. Guild, to
have allowed an open attack upon his
character to pass, without reprehension;
or the unwary to be misled into a wrong
opinion of him, by partial information.
But, while he clears a Name from obloquy,
                                    which

which ought to have been mentioned with honour, he would alfo himfelf avoid the extreme of unbounded panegyric. Even the truth of character may be injured, by exaggerated praife.

It is not to be fuppofed, that Dr. Guild was without any fault or imperfection. Infirmities are infeparable from human nature; and to be the beft of the fpecies, is only to have the feweft, and moft harmlefs defects. " For there is not a juft man up- " on earth, who doth good, and finneth " not." But if piety, and charity, and beneficence, deferve to be praifed, the claim of *Doctor Guild*, to very high commendation, cannot juftly be difputed. Opinion may fometimes ufurp the place of reafon, and honour the unworthy, even tyrants and oppreffors, with an excellent name;

but

but what are the idols of caprice and flat-
tery?

    —Doſt thou demand a teſt,
A teſt at once infallible and ſhort,
Of real greatneſs? That man greatly lives,
Whate'er his fate or fame, who greatly dies;
High-fluſh'd with hope, where Heroes ſhall deſpair.

THE END.

EXPLANATORY NOTES,

AND

OBSERVATIONS,

Indicated by the Marks of Reference, in some of the preceding pages.

Note [A] page 22.

When the Reformation took place in Scotland, a plan for the worſhip and government of the church was drawn up, embraced, and ratified, ſo far as circumſtances would permit. Of that plan, which *K. James* became afterwards ſo deſirous to alter, he had expreſſed the higheſt approbation, and given it a comparative preference, in very ſtrong terms. "I praiſe God," ſaid he, "that I " was born in ſuch a time of the light of the goſ- " pel; and to ſuch a place, as to be King of a " country where there is a church, the ſincereſt

H   " upon

" upon earth, even the church of *Geneva* not ex-
" cepted, **feeing** *they* keep feftival days, **as** *Eafter*
" and *Chriftmas.* What have they for them?
" **They** have no inftitution. As for our neigh-
" **bours in** *England*, their fervice is an ill mumbled
" Mafs in Englifh; they want little of the Mafs,
" but the liftings.

" Now I charge you, my good people (he ad-
dreffed himfelf to the General Affembly in 1590)
" Barons, Gentlemen, Minifters, and Elders, that
" you **all** ftand.to your purity, and **exhort the**
" people to do the fame; and fo long as I have
" **life and** crown, I fhall maintain the fame againft
" all deadly."

He feems to have been of the fame fentiments,
when he faid, " The religion profeffed in this
" country, wherein I was brought up, and ever
" made profeffion of, and wifhes my Son ever to
" continue in the fame, **as the** only true form of
" God's worfhip, &c.—(Bafil. Dor.) I do equally
" love and honour the learned and grave men of
" either of thefe opinions, that like better of the
" fingle form of policy in our church, than of the
" many ceremonies **of the church of England,**
" &c.—

" &c—(ib.) I exhort my Son to be beneficial to
" the good men of the Miniftry, praifing God
" that there is prefently a fufficient number of
" good men of them in this kingdom, and yet are
" they all known to be againft the form of the
" Englifh Church."

His Majefty, however, was not remarkable for
fteadinefs or confiftency. In what he now devifed,
with regard to the church of Scotland, he depart-
ed from the principles, which he had fo freely
and folemnly avowed; and zealoufly contended
for thofe very obfervances, which he had formerly
pronounced unfcriptural. But the Clergy, who
were in general, as he had faid, *againft the form of
the Englifh Church*, though difpofed to make fome
conceffions for the fake of peace, could not be
brought to an entire acquiefcence in his fcheme.

The affembly at *St. Andrews* fo far complied
with his views, as to appoint " the Holy Com-
" munion to be given feverally to every man out
" of the Minifter's hand;" and alfo, that it fhould
be " adminiftred to any fick perfon, earneftly de-
" firous of it, and known to be unable to refort
" to the church, there being fix perfons at leaft

H 2   " prefent

" prefent with the fick perfon to receive." But,
with regard to the articles, which afterwards occafioned fo much difturbance, the Affembly refolved, " to write to his Majefty, in all humility,
" to hold them excufed in that they had not
" granted thefe Articles, and to promife to travel
" for farther information to give his Majefty fatis-
" faction, fo far as in them lay."

Note [B] page 46.

King *William the Lion* was the founder of this
building, and the tradition is, that it was occafionally the place of his Majefty's refidence. It became afterwards a convent of the *Trinity Friars,*
who feem to have been eftablifhed in Aberdeen at
a very early period. Upon the fuppreffion of
monafteries at the Reformation, it had been granted, or fold to a private perfon ; and it was purchafed by Dr. Guild, in 1631, from *Mowat of
Ardo.*

In the public hall, there is a large, but rudely
                                            executed

executed portrait of William the Lion, together
with one equally large, and much more nicely
finished, of Dr. Guild. Here also are the por-
traits of most of the Patrons, from Dr. Guild to
the late reverend Dr. George Campbell; and of
some eminent Artificers, particularly one of the
father of Dr. Guild.

In this hall, the several corporations assemble,
at different times, to hold their courts, in which
the Deacon of each corporation presides. The
Convener, Deacons, and certain representatives
from the corporations, form what is called the
Convener Court, which meets in the same place.

About the year 1771, the corporations, con-
sidering that the Widows of Tradesmen were
often left in indigent circumstances, without any
suitable provision for their subsistence after their
husbands death, resolved to raise and establish a
fund, for a provision for all their widows. Articles of a scheme were accordingly prepared,
examined, and sanctioned by the corporations,
entitling the widows of the original members and
contributors to this fund, to enter thereto at the
term of Whitsunday 1778, or at the first term of

II 3   Whitsun-

Whitfunday or Martinmas thereafter, after their hufbands death ; and entitling the widows of all future entrants into any of the corporations, to an annuity out of the forefaid fund, at the firft term of Whitfunday or Martinmas after their hufbands death, and after the elapfe of feven years from their hufbands admiffion into any of the corporations. This fund, though the annuities which it can afford have not hitherto been very ample, nas been of confiderable fervice to thofe, for whom it was principally defigned.

Befides the general funds, in which the united corporations have a common intereft, there are funds peculiarly appropriated to each corporation.

Of thefe, one of the moft confiderable, belongs to the corporation of *Tailors*. It was bequeathed to them, by a perfon of the name of *Milne* (who had been a member of that corporation) and is declared to be " for the ufe and behoof of the " fons of decayed freemen of the *Tailor Trade* — " for inftructing them in *reading, writing* and *ac-* " *compting,* and *binding them apprentices* to trades " within the burgh of Aberdeen—the names of " *Milne* and *Lilly* to be preferred."

Mr,

Mr. Milne gave, by his will, an eventual interest in this fund, to the other corporations; their right to which they renounced, for what was thought an equivalent, so that the corporation of Tailors have now exclusively the benefit of the fund, for the sons of Tailors. It is appointed to be under the management of " the Patron of the " Trades' Hospital, with seven of the most judi-" cious of the Tailor trade, whereof the present " Deacon for the time one."

Note [c] page 52.

King *James* urged this Assembly by a letter, not of the most gracious kind, to an immediate and full compliance with his views. He repro-bated the proceedings of the former **Assembly,** held at *St. Andrews* in November 1617; expres-sed his high displeasure at the opposition, with which the proposed articles had hitherto met; his opinion, that much of it was owing to the indis-cretion and pusillanimity of the clergy; his **having**

H 4 once

once refolved, that he fhould never again fubmit
the matter to their judgment, knowing his right
to appoint fuch things without their confent;
and, in fhort, his fixed purpofe to be fatisfied with
nothing lefs than " a fimple and direct accepta-
" tion of the articles, in the form in which they
" were fent."

When this letter was read in the Affembly, it
gave no fmall offence to many of the members.
Even the Archbifhop of St. Andrews, who acted
as Moderator, in opening the bufinefs, profeffed
his diflike to the innovations propofed; but recommended a compliance, on account of his Majefty's earneftnefs, and to prevent the evils which
were likely to arife from any further oppofition.
Dr. Young, Dean of Winchester, his Majefty's High
Commiffioner, being requefted to give his opinion,
endeavoured, in a modeft and conciliatory fpeech,
to imprefs the affembly with a fenfe of the piety
and goodnefs of the Sovereign, and of his anxious
defire to promote the interefts of religion, and
the profperity of the national church.   The reverend Commiffioner expreffed, in the ftrongeft
terms, his own affectionate attachment to Scotland,

his

his native country ; and entreated the aſſembly, as they valued its peace and happineſs, to accept the articles, as now laid before them.

Theſe articles were; " 1, That the ſacrament " of the *Lord's Supper* be celebrate by the people " on their knees. 2, That it be privately admini- " ſtrated to perſons on death-bed, three or four " being preſent to communicate with them, and a " place convenient, and all things neceſſar de- " cently provided. 3, That *Baptiſm,* when great " need ſhall compel, be adminiſtrate in private " houſes, and declaration made thereof next " Lord's day in the congregation. 4, That Mini- " ſters catechiſe all young children of eight years " of age, and that the Biſhops, in their viſitations, " cauſe preſent them to them, and bleſs them " with prayers and impoſition of hands. 5, That " the days of our Lord's Birth, Paſſion, Reſur- " rection, and Aſcenſion, and ſending down of " the Holy Ghoſt, be obſerved by the Miniſters, " in commemoration of theſe ineſtimable bene- " fits."

It was urged in oppoſition, " That the Aſſembly " had not been regularly convened ; that there " was

" was no freedom of decifion, and that the things
" propofed were fcandalous, fuperftitious, and
" altogether contrary to the purity of the gofpel;
" That it was Idolatry, to receive the facrament
" of the *Lord's Supper* kneeling; that the admi-
" ftration of *Baptifm* out of the church was
" abufive, and favoured the opinion of the abfo-
" lute neceffity of baptifm; that the Confirmation
" of children, by the impofition of the hands of
" the Bifhop, was a Popifh facrament; that it was
" contrary to the nature of the communion, to
" celebrate it any where but in the church; and
" that the obfervation of Feafts was a Jewifh fu-
" perftition."

The articles, however, after much debate, obtained the fanction of the Affembly. But, the
general prepoffeffion againft them, remained as
ftrong as ever. They were rendered ftill more
unpopular, **by an** act of the Privy Council, which
required **a more** ftrict and folemn obfervance of
the Feftivals, **than** the Affembly had appointed;
enacting, that there fhould be *a ceffation and ab-
ftinence from all kind of labour and handy-work, upon
them;* and certifying tranfgreffors, that they
fhould

ſhould " be repute, holden, and eſteemed as ſe-
" ditious, factious and unquiet perſons, diſturb-
" ers of the peace and quiet of the Kirk, con-
" temners of his Majeſty's juſt and royal com-
" mandment, and puniſhed therefore in their
" perſons and goods, with all rigour and extre-
" mitie, to the terrour of others, at the arbitri-
" ment of the Lords of the Privie Council."

Ratiſn. of the Acts of Gl. Aſſy. at Perth, the
21ſt of October 1618.

Note [D] page 66.

A ſcene appeared, of a very different aſpect;
which exhibited to the nations of the earth, an
awful leſſon of inſtruction. To Sovereigns, it
held forth the danger of exerciſing a deſpotic
authority; and to ſubjects, the miſery of depart-
ing from thoſe neceſſary rules of ſubmiſſion, which
it is not leſs their intereſt than their duty to obſerve.

Should length of time have weakened the im-
preſſion of the ſad cataſtrophe, by which this leſ-

fon

son was conveyed; it has been renewed to the present age, by another dreadful example, with additional circumstances of distress and horror. If indeed a warning can be received by men, of which the impression shall remain indelible, it has certainly been given, by the terrible events of the Revolution in France. Unparalleled in its destructive progress, it has not only shed torrents of blood, in the unhappy country which gave it rise, but extended its atrocities to distant nations; threatened to cast down every throne, to dissolve all the bonds of social order, and to extirpate religion, peace, and liberty.

Be wise now therefore, O ye kings; be instructed, ye judges, and all ye inhabitants of the earth. Forget not truths, the remembrance of which is essential to the safety of empires. Cultivate that righteousness, by which you are assured of honour and happiness; and avoid those sins and vices, which make men uneasy in themselves, and troublesome to others; which are the misery of every private person, and the bane of public society.

Note

Note [E] page 66.

Charles I. Parl. 2. Act 5.

" Anent the Ratification of the *Covenant,* &c.
" At *Edinburgh,* June 11th, 1640.

" The Estates of Parliament, presently convee-
" ned by his Majesty's special authority, conside-
" ring the supplication of the General Assembly
" at *Edinburgh,* the 12th of *August* 1639, to his
" Majesty's High Commissioner, and the Lords
" of his Majesty's Honourable Privy Council;
" and the Act of Council the 30th of *August*
" 1639, containing the answer of the said suppli-
" cation, and the Act of the said General As-
" sembly, ordaining, by their ecclesiastick con-
" stitution, the subscription of the *Confession of*
" *Faith* and *Covenant* mentioned in their sup-
" plication; and withal having supplicated his
" Majesty, to ratify and enjoin the samen by his
" royal authority, under all civil pains, as tending
" to the glory of God, preservation of religion,
" the King's Majesty's honour, and the perfect
" peace of this kirk and kingdom, do ratify and
" approve

" approve the faid fupplication, act of Council,
" and act of Affembly; and conform thereto or-
" dain and command the faid *Confeffion* and *Cove-*
" *nant* to be *fubfcribed* by all his Majefty's fubjects,
" of what rank and quality foever, *under all civil*
" *pains;* and ordain the faid fupplication, act of
" Council, and act of the Affembly, with the
" whole *Confeffion* and *Covenant* itfelf, to be infert
" and regiftrate in the acts and books of parlia-
" ment; and alfo ordain the famen to be prefen-
" ted at the entry of every parliament, and be-
" fore they proceed to any other act, that the
" fame be publickly read and fworn by the whole
" members of parliament, claiming voice therein;
" otherwife the refufers to fubfcribe and fwear
" the fame, fhall have no place nor voice in par-
" liament: and fuch like ordain all judges, ma-
" giftrates, or other officers, of whatfoever place,
" rank or quality, and minifters at their entry, to
" fwear and fubfcribe the famen *Covenant.*"

The article of the *Covenant,* which was at the
firft fubfcription referred to the determination of
the *General Affembly,* being now determined; and
thereby *the Five Articles of* Perth, *the government*

of the Kirk by Bishops, and *the civil places and power of Kirkmen*, **upon** the reasons and grounds contained in the acts of the *General Assembly*, declared to be **unlawful** within the Kirk of *Scotland*; **all** subscriptions were expresly required to be, according to this determination.

Note [F] page 70.

In 1494 the village of Old Aberdeen was, at the desire of the King, erected, by the Pope's Bull, into an *Universitas studii generalis*, in the common form of universities, and with all the privileges competent to any of them. King *James the fourth*, in consequence of that bull, erected Old Aberdeen (1498) into a City and University, with all the privileges of the Universities of Paris, St. Andrews, and Glasgow. Within this university, Bishop *William Elphinston* founded, and amply endowed a college (1500) which was at first called *St. Mary's;* but, being afterwards taken into the

King's

King's particular protection, was for that reason called the *King's College*.

When the Reformation of religion took place in Scotland, this event brought along with it a laudable zeal for promoting useful knowledge, which appeared in the care taken by the King and Parliament, not only to increase the revenues of the universities already established, and to purge them from such particulars in their statutes, as favoured popery, but likewise to multiply seminaries of learning.

Some of the tiends, or revenues of the suppressed monasteries, having been granted to *Earl Marischal*, his lordship applied this grant to the useful purpose, of founding and endowing a college in New Aberdeen, which was called, in honour of the founder, *Marischal College*.

The charter of King Charles the first, which united this seminary to the King's College, was issued in 1641, and expresses his Majesty's intention, in the following words; " Mandavimus " quibusdam ex nobilitate aliisque, perscrutare et " iniquirere presenti statu Univ. Veteris Aber- " doniæ, et nostræ Academiæ ejusdem, nec non

" Novæ

" Novæ Academiæ Aberdonenfis, Academiæ
" Marefcallanæ nuncupatæ — — Unimus et
" erigimus dictas Academias, Veteris et Novæ
" Aberdoniæ, in Unam Univerfitatem, omni tem-
" pore futuro, *Univerfitatem* **Caroli** *Regis de Aber-*
" *dene* nuncupandam."

An inquiry was accordingly made, in terms of
this charter, into the ftate of the two colleges, by
the Earl of Sutherland and the other Commiffioners. Upon whofe report, the union was confirmed; and his Majefty granted to the Univerfity
the revenue of the Bifhop of Aberdeen; two
thirds to the King's College, and one third to the
Marifchal College. The grant was ratified by act
of parliament; and the union, in fome refpects,
took place. A Chancellor, Rector, and other
univerfity-officers, were chofen by the members
of both colleges, in joint affembly at King's College; and they appointed a common Factor, for
collecting and managing the Bifhop's rents. As
to the management of their former revenue, their
courfe of teaching, and other particulars, the two
colleges, like thofe in the Englifh Univerfities,
ftill remained diftinct and feparate.

I

It

It is probable, the colleges would have derived more benefit, than they did, from his Majefty's patronage, had not his fubfequent misfortunes in-tervened.   Nor did they long enjoy the addition, which he thus made to their revenue, by the grant of the Bifhop's rents.   Upon the reftoration of Charles the fecond, all the acts of the parlia-ments 1640, 41, &c. unfavourable to Epifcopacy, were refcinded, the Hierarchy was reftored ; and all acts, gifts, or deeds, in prejudice of the feveral Bifhoprics, were annulled.   The grant to the Colleges, and the royal charter of union connected with it, were hereby rendered void ; and the two feminaries became, feparate and diftinct, as they had been formerly.

<hr>

Note [G] page 85.

The Council of *Conftance* was one of the greateft General Councils, which the Church of Rome ever held.   It was diftinguifhed, by the perfonal prefence of *John the XXIII*, who had been elect-

ed

ed Pontiff in the year 1410; of the *Emperor Si-gifmund*; of a great number of electoral and other fovereign Princes, Cardinals, Prelates, Doc-tors, and Ambaffadors from the chief Potentates and ftates of Europe, whofe monarchs or regents could not perfonally attend.

This famous council was opened, on the fifth of November 1414, and clofed on the twenty fecond of April 1418; having lafted almoft three years and a half. It had not been long affembled, when the event took place, which occafioned the folemn proteft and appeal, of the ftates of Bo-hemia and Moravia, refpecting *John Hufs* and *Jerome of Prague;* the original of which is fup-pofed to have been the manufcript, which Doctor Guild had fo carefully preferved, and which he bequeathed to the College of Edinburgh.

The caufe of that appeal, about which fome may be defirous to have further information, was, in brief, as follows.

John Hufs, Paftor of the church of Bethlehem in Prague, Dean and Rector of the Univerfity, a man of exemplary piety and great knowledge, having incurred the difpleafure and cenfures of

I 2

the

the Archbifhop of Prague, and likewife of the Pope, for having fpoken rather freely of the See of Rome, was accufed of herefy, and fummoned to appear at Conftance, to anfwer for his conduct.

Confcious of the integrity of his heart; confiding in the goodnefs of his caufe; and thinking himfelf fecured from the malicious defigns of his enemies, by a paffport which he had received from the Emperor Sigifmund, Hufs appeared before the council, and completely refuted the charge brought againft him.

But the enemies of this good man, who were very numerous, perfifted in accufing him; and urged their complaints with fuch artifice and fuccefs, that, by the moft infamous breach of public faith, he was caft into prifon, declared a Heretic, becaufe he refufed to plead guilty againft the dictates of his confcience, and condemned to be burnt alive.

He heard his fentence with great compofure; and kneeling down in the council, he looked earneftly towards heaven, and faid, with all the fpirit of primitive martyrdom, " May thy infinite " mercy, O my God, pardon this injuftice of my " enemies.

" enemies. Thou knoweſt the injuſtice of my
" accuſers; how deformed with crimes I have been
" repreſented; how I have been oppreſſed by
" worthleſs witneſſes, and a falſe condemnation :
" Yet, O my God, let that mercy of thine, which
" no tongue can expreſs, prevail with thee not
" to avenge my wrongs."

The dreadful puniſhment, to which he was condemned, he endured, with aſtoniſhing magnani-
mity and reſignation, upon the ſixth day of July
1415; expreſſing in his laſt moments the nobleſt
ſentiments of love to God, and the moſt triumph-
ant hope of the accompliſhment of thoſe precious
promiſes, with which the goſpel animates the true
Chriſtian in the proſpect of eternity.

Jerome of Prague ſhared the ſame fate, with like
pious fortitude, on the thirtieth day of May 1416.
He had been the early and intimate companion
of John Huſs, and came voluntarily to the Council of Conſtance, with the generous deſign of ſup-
porting and ſeconding his perſecuted friend.

Jerome ſuffered extremely, in a long and rigo-
rous impriſonment; and at laſt underwent a trial,
as partial and unjuſt as that of Huſs. When he

deſired

defired to make his defence, and was refuſed per-
miſſion, he is ſaid to have exclaimed in the council,
" What barbarity is this! For three hundred and
" forty days have I been through all the variety of
" priſons.   There is not a miſery, there is not a
" want, which I have not experienced.   To my
" enemies you have allowed the fulleſt ſcope of
" accuſation ; to me, you deny the leaſt opportu-
" nity of defence.   Not an hour will you indulge
" me in preparing for my trial.   You have ſwal-
" lowed the blackeſt calumnies againſt me.   You
" have repreſented me as an Heretic, without
" knowing my doctrine ; as an enemy to the faith,
" without knowing what faith I profeſſed ; as a
" perſecutor of prieſts, before you could have an
" opportunity of underſtanding my ſentiments on
" that head.   You are a General Council ; in
" you centre all that this world can communicate
" of gravity, wiſdom, and ſanctity ; but ſtill you
" are men, and men are ſeducible by appearances.
" The higher your character is for wiſdom, the
" greater ought your care to be not to deviate in-
" to folly.   The cauſe I now plead, is not my
" own cauſe ; it is the cauſe of men, it is the cauſe
                                                " of

" of Chriſtians ; it is a cauſe, which is to affect " the rights of poſterity, however the experiment " is to be made in my perſon."

Many of the zealots, in the Aſſembly, were againſt his being allowed to proceed. It was, however, decided by the majority, that he ſhould be fully heard. He then addreſſed the Council, in ſuch a ſtrain of moving eloquence, that the hard heart of intolerant zeal ſeemed to relent, and the mind of ſuperſtition to admit a ray of conviction. A Roman Catholic hiſtorian is impartial enough to declare, " that Jerome, in all he ſpoke, ſaid no- " thing unbecoming a great and wiſe man ;" and, he candidly owns, that, " if what Jerome ſaid was " true, he was not only free from capital guilt, " but from the ſmalleſt blame."

He received, however, the ſame ſentence, which had been paſſed upon his martyred countryman.

The cruel murder of theſe two excellent men, together with ſome other provocations, occaſioned a long and bloody war, in which the Bohemians and Moravians ſhowed that determined reſolution, which their proteſt had before announced.

Addition

Addition to Note [B]

Containing, **by** desire, the particulars of *Dr. Guild's* original *Deed of Foundation* of the *Trinity* or *Trades Hospital,* **and** other articles, of **peculiar** importance **to the** Corporations of Aberdeen.

The introduction to this deed is, in the terms already mentioned (page 48) after which it **proceeds, in the** following **words ;**

' **I ordain** an preacher of the Divine Word
' at Aberdeen (whom the fix Trades fhall choofe
' **of** the number of their own paftors) with the
' Deacon Convener, Patron [of the Hofpital] who
' fhall affociate to themfelves, fix Deacons of good
' fame, prudence, and piety (one of every trade)
' whom they fhall bind with a folemn oath, one
' **by one,** that they nominate thofe whom they
' judge worthy to be prefented and admitted, **of**
' which number it fhall be leefome to the forefaid
' Minifter, with the Deacon Convener, to admit
' **him** who fhall feem moft worthy to them, and
' approved pious and fober to others, not for fup-
' plication **or** price, but only out of charity, as
' they

' they fhall anfwer to God in the day of their
' appearance."

" **Siklike**, that there be an care had of the
' Edifice, of the yearly income thereof, and of
' thofe that fhall be admitted into the faid Hofpital,
' **I ordain**, that the fame day in which the Dea-
' con Convener is chofen, the Director, Mafter or
' Guider of the faid Hofpital be chofen by the faid
' Minifter, Deacon Convener, and other Deacons,
' an diligent and godly man, able to exercife the
' office, and who fhall give an account of his dili-
' gence, care, and faithful adminiftration, to the
' faid Minifter, Deacon Convener, and other Dea-
' cons of the Trades, the week preceding the elec-
' tion of the Deacon Convener, or Deacons yearly.

' **I will alfo**, that no Woman dwell in the
' faid Hofpital (although the wife of him that is
' admitted) or ftay any time therein ; neither that
' one who is admitted, wander through the town
' or ftreets forth thereof, and that they all be
' clothed with gowns of a decent colour. **More-**
' **over**, that the faid Bead-men be fubject and
' obedient to the commands and admonifhments
' of the faid Director ; and that there be an ho-
' neft,

'neft, godly, and peaceable converfation: And
'if any of them wander without, or be trouble-
'fome within to any of their conforts, or commit
'any other fault, or be found difobedient, or any
'breaker of the fanctions of thefe mortifications,
'he fhall be punifhed in his perfon, or removed
'from the hofpital, or otherwife withdrawn by
'the Director, who in that cafe fhall take the
'advice and confent of the faid Minifter and Dea-
'con Convener; who have, and by thir prefents
'fhall have power, one poor man dying, or re-
'moving from the faid hofpital, or otherwife with-
'drawn, to choofe and put in another as afore-
'faid.

'I will alfo, that they be prefent to the Sun-
'days and weekly fermons (unlefs they be con-
'fined to their beds by ficknefs), as alfo the public
'morning and evening prayers; and alfo that in
'their own home there be an portion of the word
'of God read daily, and prayers, by a convenient
'reader, to be chofen by the Patron (who fhall
'have fifty merks paid him therefore yearly) to
'wit, the fervice to be betwixt nine and ten in the
'morning or forenoon, and three and four in the
'evening

‘ evening or afternoon ; and whofoever once (ex-
‘ cept through ficknefs) fhall be abfent, let him
‘ be admonifhed ; if twice, punifhed by the Di-
‘ rector ; if thrice, removed from the hofpital.

‘ 𝕴 𝖜𝖎𝖑𝖑 𝖆𝖑𝖘𝖔, that one of the faid poor men be
‘ Janitor of the faid hofpital weekly, having the
‘ keys of the doors and gates thereof, except the
‘ keys of the private rooms ; and fhall keep this
‘ order ; Firft, in the morning, he fhall open the
‘ outmoft gate and door in the houfe and chapel
‘ at half eight hours, that they may go and hear
‘ public prayers and fermon in the church, and
‘ that fame hour fhall ring the bell a little, that, by
‘ ringing thereof, the reft being awakened may
‘ make themfelves ready for the forefaid exercifes.
‘ Moreover, that the fame Janitor ring the bell
‘ about nine hours in the morning, and three
‘ hours in the evening, to hear and fee fcriptures
‘ and prayers in the chapel, and from thence that
‘ they go to their own private rooms, and ufe their
‘ trades till eleven hours in the forenoon, and fix
‘ in the afternoon, and then convene in the com-
‘ mon hall, and by an common provider dine and
‘ fup together, the Hebdomader ftill giving thanks.

‘ 𝕳𝖆𝖛=

' Having and holding the forefaid place (of the
' Holy Trinity Brethren) with their haill houſes,
' church-yard, yards and pertinents whatſoever,
' as alſo, the lands, annual-rents, fruits, profits
' and emoluments pertaining to the ſaid mona-
' ſtery, and mortified by me, from me and my
' heirs, to the ſaids poor and their ſuceſſors, who
' ſhall be put into the ſaid hoſpital, of our **Sove-**
' **reign** Lord the King and his ſucceſſors, in perpe-
' tual elymoſyne, et ad manum mortuam for ever,
' with full power, faculty, and authority to the
' ſaid poor, by their Director of the hoſpital and
' Conſervators foreſaid, to exact, crave, uplift, and
' receive the yearly rents from the perſons due
' therefor, and failing in payment, to compel them
' by the common law; and all and ſundry other
' things **to do**, uſe and exerce, which ſhall be
' **needful and** convenient for acquiring of pay-
' ment: paying therefor yearly and daily the ſaid
' poor, and their ſucceſſors remaining in the ſaid
' hoſpital, to our King and his ſucceſſors, as alſo
' **to** the ſaid town of Aberdeen, Magiſtrates and
' inhabitants thereof, the offerings of divine pray-
' ers; reſerving to us, during all the time of our
' life-

' lifetime, the power of the patronage and direction
' in all things, as shall seem most expedient to be
' done. In testimony whereof, &c."

The Charter contains only the above particulars, extended in the usual form, and confirmed by royal authority. Though *six* Corporations be the number mentioned, in the original deed, Dr. Guild afterwards admitted a *seventh*, the Corporation of *Fleshers*, to a share in the benefit of his hospital, by an act recorded in the minutes of the Convener Court. He had reserved to himself, during his lifetime, a power of " patronage and " direction in all things, as should seem most ex-" pedient to be done;" but he left the deed of foundation the same, in its essentials, as originally framed.

An asylum having thus been provided, for indigent members of the Corporations, benevolence also exerted itself, in behalf of their Widows and children. The fund for a provision for their Widows (mentioned page 109) is supported by,

I. An yearly fixed payment of a stipulated sum, from the unappropriated funds of the Trades Hospital.

II. A

II. A grant, from the Convener Court, of all the collections and contributions, paid by Entrants, formerly for the support of the Fabric.

III. A fixed yearly payment of a stipulated sum, from the unappropriated funds of each of the several Corporations.

IV. A fixed contribution, from all the members of any of the Corporations, who were original subscribers to the scheme.

V. Contributions from all future Entrants— *viz.* **From every** Entrant into any of the separate Trades, either being a *freeman's Son,* or who has *regularly served an apprenticeship* to a member of any of the Trades, a contribution, at his admission, of the sum of *two pounds two shillings* sterling, providing he be at the time under 40 years of age; and of the sum of *three pounds three shillings* sterlg. in case he be above that age: and, from all *extraneous entrants,* not being either freemen's sons, or who have not served a regular apprenticeship, a contribution of the sum of *four pounds* sterling, in case they are not above 30 years of age; if above 30, and under 40, a contribution of the sum of *five pounds* sterling ; and if above 40, at the time

of

of their admiffion, a contribution of the fum of *fix pounds* fterling. Extraneous Entrants, **who** may happen to **be** married to freemen's daughters, are liable only in the contribution payable **by** freemen's fons and apprentices.

VI. A tax upon the marriages of contributors, **of** *one pound* fterling, for a firft marriage; *two pounds* fterling, for a fecond; and *three pounds* fterling, for a third. In cafe of a contributor marrying a widow upon the fund, he is not liable to the tax.

The Box-mafter for the time, of each of the Trades, is obliged to collect all the dues payable to the fund, from the contributors of his corporation, and to pay in the fame regularly to the Treafurer; and the Mafter **of** Hofpital, in like manner, is obliged to collect and pay the contributions, from the members of the Convener Court.

This fund is managed, by the Convener of the Trades for the time being, along with fourteen of the Contributors, chofen, two from each corporation, by the members therein acceding to the fcheme. An annual meeting of the managers

is

is appointed to be held, upon the *first Tuesday* of *May* yearly, at which they are to elect one of their number to be Treasurer, for one year **only,** who has the power of calling all meetings of **the** managers relative to the fund ; and no business is to be transacted at any meeting, without eight of **the** managers being present. Such persons **as** are in arrear to the fund, are disqualified from being elected managers, and from voting in any matter relating to it.

The money belonging to the fund is laid out, from time to time, on the purchase of lands, or upon other proper securities bearing interest, in the name of the Treasurer, and under special qualifications. It was at first allowed to accumulate for seven years ; and, from *Whitsunday* 1778 to *Whitsunday* 1788, an annuity of *five pounds* sterling was appointed to be paid, to every Widow entitled. From *Whitsunday* 1788, the whole yearly income of the fund, after deducting the necessary expence of management, became divisible among the Widows, by way of annuity; except the sum of *ten pounds* sterling yearly, which is **always** to be added to the capital stock.

I.

If any of the contributors die in arrear to the fund, leaving a **widow** entitled to an annuity, the one half of her annuity is to be deducted, until the arrear and interest due thereon be paid. In one case, the widow is not to draw any annuity from the fund, till she be at least fifty years of age; viz. if any contributor, after he is put upon the charitable funds of the Trade to which he belongs, marry a young woman, and die, leaving her a widow entitled to claim the benefit of the fund.

There are two yearly meetings of all the Con‑tributors, the one upon the last *Tuesday* of *April*, and the other upon the last *Tuesday* of *October;* when the quantum of the annuity to be paid, for the subsequent half-year, is settled; and a roll made up of the widows, from lists given in by the Deacon and Clerk of each Trade, to which the husbands of such widows belonged; which roll is signed by the Preses in presence of the meeting, and delivered to the Treasurer, with a warrant for payment of the annuities. Those widows, who do not reside in Aberdeen, must transmit to the Treasurer, at every time they draw their an-

K
nuity,

nuity, a certificate from the Minister and two Elders of the parish where they reside, of their being
alive and unmarried.

Should a Contributor incline to sink any sum
of money upon an annuity for life, on the security
of this fund, **the** managers have power to treat,
and to conclude an agreement with him. There
is also a power reserved to alter, or add to, the
original Articles, as experience may suggest the
propriety, in order to bring the scheme to greater
perfection. But all such alterations, or additions,
must previously be submitted to the consideration
of the several Corporations; and, before they
can be adopted, must have the consent and approbation, in some cases, of five of the Corporations; in other cases, of three-fourth parts of
the whole contributors.

The Managers and Treasurer have always dif-
covered a very laudable desire, to render the
fund as beneficial as possible. Every unnecessary
expence has been carefully avoided; and the
divisible produce of the fund, regularly paid to
the Annuitants.

Since the establishment of the Trades' Hospital,
the

the Corporations have received, at different times, other donations and legacies, which are placed by the Donors under the same management and inspection, as the common funds of the Hospital, though not destined to the same purpose. Of these donations, which are in general for the support and education of the Children of artificers, one of the first was given by *Mrs Jean Guild*, the Doctor's sister.

But, next to Dr. Guild himself, the person who must be considered, as the greatest benefactor to the Incorporated Trades of Aberdeen, unquestionably was *Mr. Robert Gordon*, the founder of the hospital which bears his name. He did not indeed increase the number of the funds under their management, nor enlarge their patronage; but he gave them, notwithstanding, a most important and durable testimony of his benevolent regard.

The administration of the affairs of the charitable institution, founded by Mr. Gordon, is vested in the Provost, Baillies, Town-council, and four Ministers of Aberdeen, for the time being, as Patrons and Governors; and its primary

K 2   design

defign is declared to be, " for entertaining and
" educating Male Children and Male Grand-chil-
" dren of decayed Merchants and Brethren of
" Guild [Merchant Burgeffes] of Aberdeen."

A preference is appointed, by the founder, to
be given to boys of the name of *Gordon*, of the
name of *Menzies*, and of any other name who are
his relations, " all of them being *ftill fons or grand-*
" *fons of Burghers of Guild.*"

The fons and grand-fons of " any *other perfons*,
" who are, or have been *Burghers of Guild*, and
" actual *Indwellers* within the burgh of *Aberdeen*,"
are placed next in the order of election, prefcribed
by Mr. Gordon.

After them he ranks, among thofe for whom
his hofpital was intended, " the *fons or grand-fons*
" *of Tradefmen* [Artificers] of Aberdeen, being
" Freemen and Burgeffes thereof;" with preference among them, in the fame order, as among
the fons and grand-fons of Burghers of Guild.

This is indeed a privilege of more value, to the
families of decayed and indigent members of the
Incorporated Trades, than any other to which they
have a title. Though they have not the firft, nor

even

even the fecond claim, to the benefit of the hofpital, yet applications for admiffion, from the fons or grand-fons of Burgefs Tradefmen, are very rarely unfuccefsful in the iffue.

It is now an eftablifhed rule, that the boys who are admitted muft not, at the time of their election, be under nine years of age, nor above twelve; nor can they, according to the deed of foundation, be allowed to remain in the hofpital, after the age of fixteen. But before that period, they are ge-nerally fit for bufinefs, and are put out as appren-tices to merchants, artificers, and others, accord-ing to their genius and inclination. Their ap-prentice-fee is paid, out of the funds of the Hof-pital; and if they behave well, during all the years of their apprenticefhip, the Governors are em-powered to give each of them, at the firft term after its expiration, a gratuity of five pounds fterling, to affift them in beginning trade. Hence, among many other advantages derived from this valuable inftitution, the Merchants and Incorpo-rated Trades of Aberdeen are indebted to it, for a regular fucceffion of apprentices, the moft likely, from their education and future views, to approve

them-

themselves faithful, and solicitous to deserve the approbation of their masters. Hence, it may be added, Society in general is indebted to this institution, for many useful and respectable members, who might otherwise have been, even worse than useless. Indigence, neglected and unprincipled, is dangerous to society, as well as wretched in itself.

To venerate the memory of the generous and charitable men, by whose bounty institutions have been established, which are so eminently calculated to prevent this formidable evil, and to diffuse among mankind so much good, is a tribute which grateful posterity will delight to pay. Let us honour, as we ought, the channels through which we have received such blessings. But, let us ever ascribe the glory to THE GREAT BENEFACTOR OF ALL—THE FATHER OF LIGHTS—FROM WHOM COMETH DOWN EVERY GOOD, AND EVERY PERFECT GIFT. AMEN.

THE END.

www.ingramcontent.com/pod-product-compliance
Lightning Source LLC
Chambersburg PA
CBHW020405030726
47496CB00007B/2311